.

THE DARK SIDE

ONE MAN'S JOURNEY TO THE 125 LINE AND BACK

CAPTAIN DEL STEPHENS

LUMINARE PRESS

WWW.LUMINAREPRESS.COM

The Dark Side: : One Man's Journey to the 125 Line and Back
© 2016 Del Stephens

Printed in the United States of America

Cover Design:

Luminare Press
467 W 17th Ave
Eugene, OR 97401
www.luminarepress.com

ISBN: 978-1-937303-80-8

TABLE OF CONTENTS

The Addiction Begins

I ROLLED OUT OF BED AND MADE MY WAY OUTSIDE WHERE MY father and grandfather were getting the boat ready. Still groggy and barely awake, my brother and I scrambled into the camper and soon we were off to the coast. We climbed up onto the bed area above the cab but we were too excited to go back to sleep; instead we watched for deer along the highway to the coast. It was always fun to see how many deer we could count on the two-hour ride from Corvallis to Newport through the coast range. In 1969, the highway still had plenty of deer, as well as plenty of curves on that road. Once we rolled into Newport, we'd drive through the state park overlooking the jetties to check out the offshore conditions. If there weren't any white caps and the conditions looked favorable, we'd launch the boat and soon be a few miles offshore fishing for salmon.

Fast forward about 20 years, same scenario, but this time I was towing my own boat and this would be the start of another chapter in my life—I was about to have my first experience with albacore tuna. I heard tuna were close to shore and everyone was getting them; I had to try it. I had caught tuna in Mexico but never off the coast of Oregon and never from my own boat.

It was a three-hour drive through the coast range before day-light and the plan was to make a quick stop to pick up a few tuna feathers (see page 44) from one of the locals, and then hopefully my buddy and I would be running offshore in no time. But as luck would have it, the best laid plans sometimes get derailed. The local tackle guy was a no-show, so after waiting for over an hour, we decided to run offshore anyway and see what we could do. I figured tuna were predator-type fish and some of the lures I used for mackinaw lake trout should work. The local marina store gave us some coordinates and said, "Just run to this location and you'll see the fleet of boats and you should be in the fish." Could it be that easy?

We were greeted with a glassy smooth ocean and it was a quick 20 miles to the coordinates we were given but it was a lonely ocean with no boats in sight. I scanned the horizon with binoculars, looking for the fleet, when my buddy mentioned there were fish jumping beside the boat. Amazingly, we had found the tuna but the fleet of boats was nowhere to be found, so we decided to try our luck and started deploying the large mackerel-style plugs.

Wham! The first rod went off before I could even get it in the rod holder and halfway through a blistering run I began to hear the sound of metal disintegrating right in my hands. The drag was toast and now I was forced to use my thumb for a drag. A few short runs later and I had the fish up next to the boat, going around and around in what I would eventually come to know as the tuna death spiral. It was wild pandemonium and my buddy's white shorts soon turned to pink from the blood bath that ensued. Our heavy salmon rods handled the fish just fine but the reels were no match for the incredible blistering runs the tuna made when they exploded on the plugs. We soon had eight nice fat tuna onboard, four reels that were pretty much wasted, and with our cooler stuffed, we decided to stop. Smiling and laughing at what had just happened, we rinsed the boat out and headed back to port. It wasn't even noon yet and normally you'd think if you missed the first light bite, things would be slow, but these silver bullets hit everything we put overboard. Of course it was also mid-July, and folks around here in the Pacific Northwest have a saying I've come to know well, "Anyone can catch a tuna in July." So true that day, as we were living proof.

Fast forward another 20 years and you will have heard many stories from fishermen with similar experiences getting their first taste of this incredible fishery. (By the way, when I say "fishermen," that includes women who fish, too.) Throughout the late 1900s, Chinook salmon was king of the saltwater in the Pacific Northwest, but declining runs of Chinook and coho in the late 90s and early 2000s left offshore anglers looking for something else to chase. Albacore have been available and harvested by commercial fishermen for quite some time but only in the last few years have a handful of sport fishermen realized they were out there. Albacore move into the waters off northern California, Oregon, and Washington as the summer currents from the south push the warm temperatures above 58 degrees. Typically, July 4th signals the start of the season and anglers go looking running 40-60 miles offshore.

The early part of the season is extraordinary by any standards and is what gets beginners addicted to the fishery. The singing of line screaming off reels with multiple fish hitting simultaneous doubles, triples, and quads is to tuna anglers what a hit of cocaine is to drug addicts. Except that tuna anglers have to wait all winter and spring to get their fix. But that first fix of the season is the beginning and the end. It's the beginning of the offshore tuna season and the end to what spouses know of their partners until late fall when the season comes to an end and the anglers sulk back into their semi-normal state. They will then spend their days reminiscing about their best trip and in some cases, to get away from the chill of the Northwest, they will think of a mid-winter trip somewhere warm where they hope to do battle with something on the end of a stout rod that will wet their thirst for some salty action.

To say that what has happened to anglers in the waters of the Northwest is a fad, would be a gross understatement. It is the fastest growing fishery on the West Coast by any standards. Our fellow anglers to the south have been chasing tuna for many years and for the most part we are late to the dance but are getting there nevertheless.

When you mention albacore on the West Coast, most people think of Southern California. But things are constantly changing in the offshore fisheries and with liberal limits in Oregon and no limits in Washington, there are days when the bite is so hot you could boat 100 fish by noon, that is, if you had the storage and ice capacity. It's not too uncommon for four anglers to bring home 40 plus fish the first few times until they realize they can't eat all those fish and start imposing self-limits just to be able to get another chance to run offshore for another fix.

The albacore fishery off Oregon and Washington is very healthy and has seen a strong increase in the numbers of fish in the last 10 years. Recreational anglers, even in spite of the liberal limits, take less than 1% of the overall harvest, leaving commercial boats from Oregon, Washington, California, Canada, and Hawaii to take the bulk of the annual harvest.

Tuna anglers are a different breed. They come from all walks of life and they've all taken a different path to tuna fishing. Most are salmon anglers who have been offered a ride by a friend and once they get a taste of the action, well, it's "Welcome to the Dark Side." They're hooked and the addiction begins. It's been compared to a cocaine addiction but twice as expensive. They spend $100,000-$3,000,000 on a boat depending on the severity of the fever and buy half a dozen $800 rods with gold reels for trolling. Then August comes around and they realize they need more gear because the fish decided to change feeding habits and now the anglers are cussing and swearing because nothing they've learned is working. They go online to order more gear then have it shipped to their buddy's house so the spouse doesn't see it, hoping they can also intercept the credit card bill before it's seen. Step two of the education and the advanced stages of addiction are becoming more apparent. The signs are obvious; they are constantly checking chat forum websites for a live report or checking the weather forecast for the next opportunity to run offshore. If the ocean is too rough, they could be grumpy and in a foul mood resembling coming down off a drug high.

Tournament time gives them the opportunity to rub elbows with fellow addicts, swap stories, place side bets, and throw smack talk at fishermen from rival ports. The testosterone runs high and the egos sometimes get out of control only to get put back in place or humbled in the event of a poor showing on game day. It's all in good fun as tuna anglers are a friendly bunch. They like each other and hate each other depending on the day and the time. They'll also be the first to drop everything and run to help each other when a fellow tuna junkie has an emergency 50 miles offshore. Loyalty for a fellow addict is a common thread you'll find among them.

Their playground is far from land and the first few times going out that far can be a little scary as they lose sight of civilization. Although the action on this playground is anything but civilized—blood is flying everywhere and the anglers come home looking like they've been at war. They throw their clothes away and start looking for old clothes that haven't been worn in years. Tuna clothes—a whole new category of clothing. And they don't bother asking their spouse to go shopping for them because the spouse won't have a clue where to find that type of attire, which is right there in the anglers' closet all along.

In just a few short weeks, the tournaments are over and the camaraderie and stories will have to carry them through till the next season. This scenario will continue to be played out over and over throughout the month of July and into early August until they ply their tactics and return to port some day with little to show for their effort. The fish are still there but have now changed feeding habits and it's time to change strategies This is where the seasoned anglers continue to bring home the bounty while the beginners or "tuna newbies" either learn a new method or troll endlessly in hopes their tactics will still work. Some will go home to pursue other species while others will still have the need for the fix and will learn to jig iron, pitch swimbaits, or fish live bait.

You'll know the ones who've been addicted for years because they've mellowed and have gotten used to the ups and downs of the bite and have learned a few tricks along the way. They're the quiet ones who come in from a tough day on the water and still have the grin as well as a boatload of fish, leaving the newbies to wonder what they were doing wrong.

Once tuna anglers get that last fix in and decide to hang it up for the season they'll have eight months to shop tackle, peruse catalogs, go to sport shows, climb all over their next new boat during boat shows, and go to a few TA (Tuna Aholics) meetings. At first wives may frown at the thought of having their husbands going to anything referenced as "TA" but once they realize it's to help with the husbands' addiction, they'll gladly send the husbands on their way in hopes of getting their other husbands back—the ones the wives knew before the first tuna trip. Just like addicts though, wives won't know the TA meetings aren't intended to cure the addiction, just keep it pacified until the next season. You know how junkies with an addiction are, they'll say anything just to keep getting to do the same thing.

Spouses don't know it but tuna anglers will never be the same. The partners they married are now forever changed. They'll just have to get used to hearing the strange phrases used by fellow addicts. It's like Morse code but geared for offshore. Examples include "swimbait on the drop back," "whack 'em and stack 'em," "tuna virgin," "working the iron," "running to the blue water," "green water hogs," and the list goes on.

"Tuna addicts" start watching online sea surface websites waiting for the warm water in Northern California to form a solid connection to the warm water off Oregon and Washington creating "Tuna Alley" or the "Tuna Highway." Once that has occurred and is within a reasonable distance offshore, it's time to run offshore after the fish. Just a few short years ago, a reasonable distance to run for most northwest anglers would've been 35–40 miles in their pursuit of halibut but today "reasonable" is anything within 75 miles. I still remember that first time I ran 90 miles one way then came back to port and proceeded to the fuel dock and replaced the $800 worth of fuel I burned. On occasion, the warm water will swing in within 10-15 miles of the shore and a few more salmon anglers will get a taste of what it's like to catch a sports car with a fishing rod—and their lives will change forever. "Welcome to the Dark Side," we say, as the addiction begins for another tuna newbie. New tuna anglers will start looking at blue water tackle online and search for a bigger boat. Aluminum boats in the 22–26 foot range no longer dominate the offshore scene and it's not uncommon to see big center consoles with triple outboards or 50 to 60-foot sportfishers. These are the kind of boats you'd expect to see on the East Coast—boats traditionally not seen much in the Northwest until recently. The need for bigger, smoother-riding offshore boats has driven many anglers to the East Coast for big center consoles with full enclosures. Hydra Sport Customs and Yellowfins are showing up, along with occasional 35 to 57-foot Bertrams, Cabos, Albemarles, Rivieras, Luhrs, and other styles not readily known in the Northwest. To say that the landscape of the offshore fishing in the Pacific Northwest is changing would be putting it mildly.

Chasing this fabulous table fare is not a complicated endeavor. You learn what to look for, wait for the warm water to show up, run offshore, and chances are you'll find these longfin silver bullets.

Some might laugh at us since we are truly novices compared to anglers farther south who have been catching tuna for years, but it's still new enough for most that we get excited to hear stories of others catching fish or of another opportunity to run to the blue water. You have to be pretty hardy to chase these guys because the summer winds on the north Pacific can be brutal, and a four-foot wind chop on a six-foot swell eight seconds apart can test the durability of any good boat as well as the endurance of any seasoned, salty fisherman. Many a good angler will sit on the sidelines and watch the weather forecast, then make plans to call in sick or take a day off from work should the need arise during the week.

Labor Day weekend is the end for some as their kids are now back in school and fall hunting is pulling them away from the coast. Spouses who have gone through a season know what to expect and are breathing a sigh of relief, as the person who resembles their significant other starts to focus back on family, school, fall football, work, etc.—the kinds of things most normal partners deal with during the year. Many of the addicts will never fully recover and soon will secretly start counting the days till they can run to the blue water. A few TA meetings will get them through the winter and they'll have their own stories to share with fellow Tuna Aholics. Life will be good.

The commercial tuna boats have been bringing these silver bullets to the docks for many years but it's only been in the last 10 years that the tuna fishery has taken off and really flourished—in part due to the attention the Oregon Tuna Classic Tournament Series has brought to the fishery. Although still very much in its infancy, the fishery is growing quickly as witnessed by the change in style of boats now cruising offshore.

My introduction to this fishery came back in the mid-1990s and in a 23-foot aluminum inboard jet sled—a boat designed for running shallow rivers with an occasional trip offshore 15-35 miles for halibut. It didn't have insulated fish boxes or a long fuel range, which worked out fine on my first adventure when chasing the fish since the ocean was like a lake and we only had to run 19 miles to get to them. We didn't have tuna feathers or clones. There was no seminar prior to this trip and frankly there was only a handful of sport guys chasing tuna in both Oregon and Washington.

On a calm ocean back then you'd be lucky to see another boat 50 miles offshore but today that has changed dramatically. You now have to keep a good watch because it can be a real zoo at times with hundreds of boats congregated on a school of fish. You may not be able to see it from the beach, but there's a lot going on just over the horizon when the ocean is flat and the winds of summer allow guys to run to the blue water.

In July 2008, "Oregon's Amazing Albacore," written by Mike Mazur for *Sport Fishing Magazine* got the attention of one of the titans of tuna fishing and Tred Barta had to come out to see what the fuss was about. He left shaking his head and commenting that the albacore fishing off the Oregon Coast was the best he'd ever seen.

The fishing was good on that trip but nothing like when the bite is wide open, you're dead in the water, and you're bringing them over the rail at a fast pace of 20-30 fish per hour. Not sure what he would have said if he'd witnessed some of the wide-open bites we experience on a regular basis.

This book will give you the information needed to catch these great game fish. But before we venture down that road and I divulge all my secrets, I'll share a little more about these sleek silver bullets and my journey to catch them.

The Species

So what's all the fuss about? Albacore tuna, *Thunnas alalunga,* is one of the most sought after fish around the world, both commercially and recreationally, and is classified as a "Highly Migratory Species" (HMS). In the United States, they are managed federally by the National Marine Fisheries Service (NMFS) in cooperation with state fish and wildlife agencies. These fish are found around the world and can travel across an entire ocean. They are sleek, torpedo-shaped, and built for speed—at times they can reach 50 miles per hour. Commonly referred to as "Silver Bullets" by us sport guys and "Chicken of the Sea" by most others, they are the easiest of all 21 tuna species to identify with their very distinct, long pectoral fin.

Albacore frequent the waters off the West Coast from Northern Mexico to Southeast Alaska. They travel across the Pacific Ocean from Japan in a counter clockwise migration and you generally have two separate migrations of fish. The southern migration visits the waters off Mexico and Southern California. The Pacific Northwest gets the northern migration of fish, which typically come across the Pacific Ocean somewhere north of the San Francisco Bay area and annually travel up the coastline many years cruising past places like Sitka, Alaska, before making the return cycle back around to Japan.

Rarely do the albacore from Southern California make it up into the Northwest although some years, yellowtail, dorado, and opah will show up. During strong El Nino years, it's not uncommon to also see marlin.

Unlike non-migratory species that are found only off our coasts, U.S. anglers are not the only ones fishing for this highly migratory species. Fisheries for species such as albacore require cooperative international management to ensure the resource is abundant and global harvests are sustainable.

Most of the albacore harvested in the U.S. comes from the Pacific, mainly from waters off the U.S. West Coast. Anglers have been harvesting this "white meat" tuna off the West Coast for more than 100 years. Because the last of the canneries in California have closed and albacore populations have shifted northward with changing oceanographic conditions, the bulk of the albacore catch now comes from Oregon and Washington. Most commercial fishermen use a trolling method of either multiple lines with multiple lures moving through the water or pole-and-line with a special jig (commonly referred to as Jack Poling) to harvest albacore. They generally fish from mid-June to as late as October 31st, depending on their location. Today, catches of albacore make up the majority of the total commercial tuna harvest off the West Coast. The catch is canned in boutique and major canneries in Oregon and Washington. Some is sold locally (some fishermen sell direct to the public), and some is shipped to major canneries outside Oregon and Washington for processing. The biggest difference between the commercial canneries of old and today's boutique canneries is the quality of the end product. The tuna caught and canned in the old style canneries is cooked twice, and generally after the first time it's cooked, it gets dried out, requiring a broth to be added to it when it goes into the can to be cooked for the second time. Tuna canned in smaller boutique canneries up and down the Northwest are typically younger tuna with less mercury content and are canned just one time in their own juices. It's not uncommon to see garlic or jalapeno added to create a unique flavor. This is the canned tuna you see in the store that's over five dollars a can versus what I grew up eating and is still available for around one dollar per can. The demand for a higher quality product is changing the commercial landscape as well as the sport.

The fish traveling along the West Coast are considered immature and are typically three to four years old and weigh 15–25 pounds early in the season and 25–35 pounds by late season. Early season in the Northwest is June and July while late season is anything from mid-August up to Halloween. Traditionally, July 4th is the date sport guys venture offshore in the hunt for tuna although during El Nino weather pattern years, it's not uncommon for the season to start sometime in mid-June. Chat forums in the Northwest really heat up in May and June leading you to believe that the tuna are here sooner, leaving tunaholics with one eye on work and the other on their favorite chat forum waiting for news of the first blood from a sport-caught fish hitting the deck. Once that ceremonious first fish has been caught, the online chatter heats up dramatically and the tuna fever that many have been afflicted with takes over.

Some years there will still be a few fish around in November but weather becomes more of a factor by then. The latest I have ever fished albacore was November 9th. The water was still plenty warm and we had a nice ocean forecast so why not ? I decided to venture offshore and see if they were still out there and can now say I've caught tuna in November.

Many years some of the best fishing is in September and October but a lot of people have shifted their focus away from tuna by then. Summer vacation is over, kids are back in school, and many are hunting something else. It's as if someone throws a switch on Labor Day to signal the change of seasons and everyone goes home, making it less crowded now for tuna anglers.

Tuna tend to be more abundant during September and October

when the seas and weather are also calmer. I would also definitely not discount November if the water stays warm. Maybe someone will catch a Thanksgiving tuna one of these days.

Some of my best days have been in October, boating 73 fish on one three-hour stop before having to quit because we ran out of ice. We left them still chewing and willing to take pretty much anything we threw over.

Late season fish will commonly top 30 pounds with an occasional fish pushing 40 pounds. They are considered mature after 5 years and can live as long as 12 years. Mature albacore are 70-100 pounds when they spawn in the Midway Islands of the South Pacific.

Bluefin and bigeye tuna commonly swim through the same waters and history tells us the Indians on Vancouver Island, B.C., hunted them near shore from their canoes. A few times during the summer someone will generally hook up with one of these monsters only to get spooled or broken off and the angler will miss out on capturing one of these giants. Local online chat forums then heat up with chatter referencing using bigger rods and heavier tackle but generally there are only one or two sightings per season. The record for the largest bluefin tuna landed by a sport angler in the Northwest is slightly over 100 pounds. Anglers on the East Coast hunt as a pack, helping each other to find these big fish. They then use the proper tackle to fight these fish, which sometimes approach 800 pounds. In the Northwest anglers are still excited just to catch a 30-pound albacore and hope to see one of these big guys cruise by. It's not impossible to land a big guy on albacore gear and as anglers become better at the sport, I suspect a larger bluefin tuna will someday show up on the docks.

FINDING FISH

THE HUNT FOR ALBACORE BEGINS LONG BEFORE YOU EVER LEAVE the dock. If you talk to seasoned albacore folks, you'll find they use a combination of techniques and tools to help them decide where they're going to begin fishing.

When I was new to this fishery, I was learning by trial and error using a few things I had learned on trips to Mexico and Central America where we chased yellowfin tuna. I have since chased a lot of different species of tuna in a lot of places and have come to realize that many of the techniques employed in one area or for a certain species will also work for albacore. I have also learned that most tuna are very similar in both their feeding habits and in the techniques that it takes to catch them. In the beginning, the learning curve was pretty steep since I didn't have anyone to teach me. Tuna seminars in the Northwest weren't even in our vocabulary back then.

Today I believe there are two key elements that you must learn if you hope to successfully catch tuna on a consistent basis.

Locating - The first thing you must learn is that locating albacore makes up 50%—half—of catching them. Let me repeat this for those of you who are reading too fast and are anxious to get on to other topics—finding albacore is 50% of catching them! I would encourage you to spend the time and effort to get really good at finding them, especially if you intend to fish during the late season when things can get more difficult. There is no shortcut to this and you need to become very proficient at recognizing the offshore signs. Sometimes they'll be obvious and other times it becomes more of an educated hunch from past experience.

14   DEL STEPHENS

Right technique - Once you've found the tuna, you need to know what technique to use to catch them on any particular day based on the conditions present. The techniques you use during the early part of the season may not work during the late season based on the conditions that are present. I should also mention there's not just one set method to catch tuna but in fact there are many ways. Just when you think you have everything dialed in, someone comes up with a new lure or technique for a specific use, or the tuna themselves throw you a curve and change things up.

We're all unique in how we approach something and we all have our own way of doing things. The technique I use may not be the method for the next person. It's more important for you to learn a method and style that works for you. Then refine it and get good at it.

When on the hunt to find fish, most tuna folks will typically run till they see some type of sign indicating tuna could be present, then deploy troll gear to find the fish. In years past, I used this method many times during the early part of the season, but now when we get into late August and on into the fall, I hardly ever troll to find the fish.

Albacore like nice clean water in the 58–62 degree temperature range and as is the case off Oregon and Washington, that generally requires a 30 to 50-mile run to find those water temperatures depending on which port you're chasing them from. The warm water currents tend to sweep closer to the southern Oregon coast making them easier to get to for those with smaller boats. That was the case for me when I ran 19 miles off Brookings that first trip.

Running 50 miles offshore is an expensive endeavor for most people and it pays to do a little research prior to the trip. Taking time to research and plan will pay huge dividends when it comes to chasing these critters. An average trip for me will burn 135 gallons; if I didn't have an idea of where to go or where to begin fishing, that could become even more expensive. I was very fortunate to have lady luck on my side that first trip offshore many years ago as I had the benefit of a reliable report from the marina store. We ran to the coordinates we were given but were surprised to find there were no other boats around. Talk about a lonely feeling when it's your first time that far offshore and not a boat in sight! Not knowing what I know today, if we hadn't seen the fish jumping, I probably would've gone looking for the fleet.

If you're new to the game and don't have much experience offshore, it will make you nervous being beyond the sight of land with no other boats in view, and instead of searching for tuna you'll be more focused on searching for other boats just to feel safe. That's okay—sometimes finding other boats is not a bad thing when you're new to the sport.

I can't stress the value of a reliable report of where fish have been caught recently. Building a reliable network of friends who are willing to share information is a great way to help each other. Joining an online chat forum such as The Salty Dogs forum on ifish. net, Coastside Fishing Club, or BloodyDecks forum on bdoutdoors. com is a great way to get good web-based sources of information. There are folks with many years of experience who will generally share tips and techniques although very few will reveal their recent or favorite fishing hole.

The traditional method to find tuna is to run offshore looking for water that is 58 degrees. Once you find that, start looking for a water temperature jump of a half a degree in a very short distance, such as a quarter to a half a mile. At the same time, you want to watch water color. You're looking for clean green or clean blue water and the transition from green to blue water is normally a very good place to start fishing. Many times the green water will hold more fish because it has a higher plankton count, which generally translates into more bait available, but fish really prefer nice, clean blue water. If you can find a blue water/green water transition area, many times the fish will move back and forth between the two areas. I can't count how many times I've started fishing in green water and after a short while, noticed we were fishing in blue water. Occasionally, you'll actually see a hard line with green water on one side and blue on the other. It will literally change from green to blue as if someone drew a line in the ocean. I've come across this a number of times over the years and it has always turned out to be a great place to fish. The tuna love good, clean blue water but they also love to eat and there's generally more food in the green water. This is where the phrase "green water hogs" comes from.

Before you get to this point in your adventure, it's a good idea to take your boat out on the water with some type of thermometer and check it against what your electronics are reading. Don't be surprised if the electronic temperature sensor is slightly off. You could end up running all over the ocean looking for the right water temperature and running right over fish while burning precious fuel.

If you perform a software update, check it again. I love my Garmin electronics but every time I update the software, the water temperatures also reset and I have to recalibrate it before heading offshore. It only takes a few minutes to perform and you're good to go again.

A great tool for finding temperature breaks is a web-based online sea surface temperature service such as Terrafin. It's a web-based service that will also show chlorophyll concentrations and plankton counts which in turn, translates into more food. Services such as this can save you hundreds of dollars in wasted fuel covering lots of ocean. It offers you the opportunity to look online the day before your trip to find where the warm water breaks are. It really helps if the information corresponds with locations where fish have been caught in the past or are known to hold tuna. A subscription to one of these web-based services is generally $99 per year. This tends to be a pretty good bargain as compared to burning hundreds of dollars' worth of fuel running around on the ocean with nothing to go on other than just cruising looking for other signs indicating tuna are present. The following chart from Terrafin.com shows water temperature. You'll notice it also shows the Longitude and Latitude grid.

Move the cursor anywhere on the chart, and the Latitude/Longitude and Temperature are displayed in the browser status window (at the bottom left side of the browser screen).

Click anywhere on the chart to first specify your origin. As you move the mouse, the distance and bearing from that origin is displayed in the browser status window. This will give you the heading to take out of your home port. It will also show you the distance you will need to travel.

A great trip-planning feature allows you to place marks or plot a route on any chart. A list of the selected waypoints is then created at the bottom of the page, which is easily printed along with the chart. This is a great pre-trip planning tool, and also a simple way to create a float plan to leave at home or with others giving them information as to where you'll be offshore!

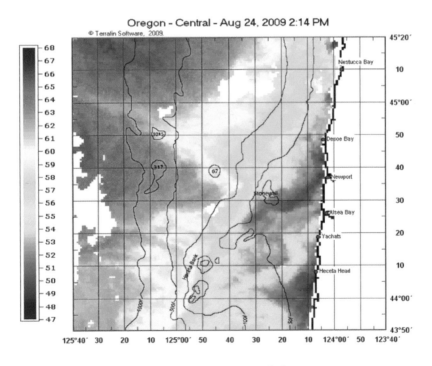

Terrafin water temperature graph from 8/24/09

Chlorophyll data, as shown in the following chart, can be used to predict the water color. High concentrations = higher nutrient (plankton) levels, but greener water color. Low concentrations = clearer, blue water. These charts have proven to be extremely valuable for both inshore and offshore fishing.

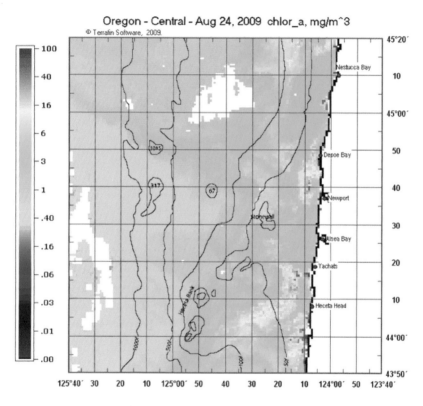

Terrafin Chlorophyll chart from 8/24/09

Ideally you're looking for a good water temperature break that also corresponds with a good chlorophyll break showing the transition from green water to blue water.

The ocean is very much like a good steelhead stream in that it has areas that are known to consistently hold fish. The ocean has a lot of different currents and when they are funneled into underwater canyons and up against sea mounds they cause upwellings and currents which flow in many different directions. In many cases, the currents and upwellings are strong enough to trap and hold bait fish which will also cause the albacore to congregate in those areas. In many situations where you find these currents you'll also find chlorophyll color changes as well as water temperature breaks. They may vary from day to day or week to week but many times they'll be in the same or close to the same places from year to year. There are always variances to this but for the most part they'll overlap on a fairly consistent basis.

Birds - Typically when you get in an area that has tuna, you'll also notice there are more birds. Tuna tend to push bait up to the surface when feeding which then allows birds to dive on the fleeing bait and on the scraps left over from the feeding tuna. Running offshore and spotting birds diving on the water is a great sign fish are present. In some cases, a group of birds setting on the water might also indicate the fish have been feeding there.

I have been offshore when there were no birds or any other signs of life and in most of those trips there weren't any tuna around either. In that situation, you have to go looking elsewhere to find the fish. There are always exceptions to everything but most of the time common sense prevails.

Traveling in packs or with a buddy boat is another good way to go looking. It's a very big ocean out there, and having another boat around can give you a little peace of mind knowing that should you have an emergency, someone is close by to assist.

Commercial boats - On one occasion, many years ago, when I was still a tuna newbie, I was running out of Newport, Oregon, and had what I considered a pretty reliable report from the guys at Englund Marine. "Head west on a heading of 270 and at 30 miles you should get into fish." The same report also mentioned if you went another 5 miles there were bigger fish. We took a heading of 270 and were soon cruising across a very flat ocean. I had a buddy boat running with me and when we were only 20 miles out we hit clean green 58-degree water. We kept going, watching the temperature, hoping for a sharp jump, but it never came and about the time we reached the 30-mile mark, we came across a group of commercial tuna boats. They were all strung out in a line and headed south. I stopped and took a moment to chat with my buddy on the other boat, discussing what to do. We hadn't seen any significant water temperature jump, nor had we seen any birds or other signs indicating tuna could be present. What would you do? Would you continue to run, looking for some sign of tuna? We decided it wouldn't hurt to put the troll gear in the water and troll for a short time just to check it out. We were still getting the gear deployed when the clickers on the reels started singing. We never went more than a half mile from that location all day. Back and forth, heading west a half mile, then back the other direction heading east. There were no boats in sight, but we had found the tuna so we kept working the same spot until the fish boxes couldn't hold any more fish and we had to stop. It was barely noon and we were plugged.

One of the best lessons I ever learned came that day. If you haven't seen any obvious signs of tuna, keep on the lookout for the commercial fleet. They make their living off the ocean and most of the time you won't find them fishing where there are no fish.

What worked in the past - What happens when you get out there and can't find the tuna? Go back to where you've caught tuna in the past. Hopefully you've saved those locations as waypoints on your electronics.

On one occasion, a friend wanted me to take a few of his work buddies fishing and he had heard a report of fish being caught in a certain location the previous day and suggested we try that spot. This was an area I traditionally don't fish but was willing to give it a try.

Once we arrived on location that morning we deployed the gear and trolled around with no action other than radio chatter during the first hour. I tried numerous things—changing gear, changing troll speed, and I even changed the direction of my troll—all to no avail. Typically, when the radio has lots of chatter, others are not catching fish either, and after two hours of nothing but radio conversations, I pulled the gear and ran 20 miles south to a location where I had caught fish earlier in the week.

We left a good sized fleet of boats, content with what they were getting, and now we were all alone with no one in sight in any direction. I pulled the throttles back and as the boat settled into the water, my crew started deploying the gear. We didn't even have three lines in the water when the first rod went off—we were hooked up. We trolled back and forth over one small patch of water the rest of the day. It wasn't great fishing but we were steadily picking them off and were definitely doing better than where we started the day. Later in the afternoon, a buddy boat came trolling by and called on the radio to inquire as to how we were doing. I indicated we were not lighting the world on fire but doing okay and asked how they were doing. They mentioned they were having a great day leaving me to wonder about making another move. Later, when we were back in port, I learned they had 6 fish for the day versus our 23 fish, which turned out to be the high boat in the port that day since most boats stuck with that first location.

Tuna places - If you're fishing out of Newport, Oregon, you might find yourself fishing "Tuna Town," which is not a spot, but more of an area, around 45N X 125W. If you run out of the Columbia River ports of Ilwaco, Washington, or one of the other Oregon ports such as Hammond or Warrenton, one of the common places where fish are found is the Astoria Canyon and a good area to try is 46.00-46.10N X 124.50-125W. Farther north out of Westport, anglers work the Willapa Canyon. There are many other places to target and getting familiar with these places can help when planning a trip offshore.

Jumpers - Generally, once you get into August and the late season, you'll start seeing jumpers. That's an obvious sign you've found the fish, and where there's one, there are more. These things travel in schools, so stop and start working them.

Using your electronics - Electronics have really come a long way in the last few years. Once you're offshore in an area where you believe there might be tuna, adjust your sonar by taking it off the auto mode and adjusting it to only look at the top 60-100 feet of water. I don't really care what's down 3,000 feet as I can't fish it anyway, so by adjusting the sonar to a shallow depth, it gives me a better picture of what's in the fishable zone under my boat.

Standard sonar sends one single frequency at a time. Since the only feedback is from this one single signal, there is little information to work with, which limits the clarity and resolution available with standard sonar.

If you have a unit that has dual frequency, set that up and use both. In many cases, that will give you a split screen. Varying frequencies are going to give you varying pictures. If you consistently fish with your sonar set up this way, you'll soon learn what the tuna look like on the screen.

CHIRP sonar - (Compressed High Intensity Radar Pulse) is the newest and latest thing in sonar technology and can really give you a sharper, clearer picture, especially when adjusted to those shallow depths. Instead of sending just one single frequency, CHIRP sends a continuous sweep of frequencies ranging from low to high. CHIRP sonar technology then interprets frequencies individually upon their return. Since this continuous sweep of frequencies provides CHIRP with a wider range of information, CHIRP sonar is able to create a much clearer, high resolution image.

In 2012, I upgraded my sonar to the CHIRP technology using Garmin's GSD26 with two through hull transducers—one for low frequencies and another for high frequencies. When I'm looking for fish, I generally have it on both frequencies using a split screen.

Turning up the gain 10%-15% will also give you a better chance of seeing thermoclines. A *thermocline* is a thin but distinct layer in which temperature changes more rapidly with depth than it does in the layers above or below. During the late season when the water temperatures climb above 62 degrees, many times you'll find the tuna down 35–60 feet, in and below the thermocline, and not too willing to come up for troll gear.

Once into the late season, I consider trolling to find fish a poor method of locating them. I look at Terrafin online to find the warm water breaks, while also checking to see if the chlorophyll breaks also line up with the temperature breaks. If that's not available, I will probably head back to where I've caught fish in the past, running offshore, and keeping an eye out for birds working the surface. I also use a Sirius weather subscription feature, which gives me sea surface temperature shading on my chartplotter that looks similar to what I use online. I can adjust the screen out to my intended fishing location to see if anything has changed which might cause me to adjust my intended target location. Keep in mind that if you haven't calibrated your temperature unit, it may not match what is being shown on the screen once you get out into the ocean. I've heard people say that their sea surface weather feature wasn't accurate. But when I asked them if they had taken the time to calibrate their temperature unit, they admitted they hadn't thought about that and because they had been catching tuna, they just thought the unit wasn't that accurate. Yet that isn't the case; it works well. The latest advancements in electronics are great, but they still require you to set things up the first time.

I generally run to my intended location and once I arrive at my destination, I'll pull the throttles back, check the sonar to see what's beneath the boat, and in many cases, just start fishing using a number of techniques. It sometimes takes a little while to get used to your equipment, but once you take it off auto and adjust it manually to see just the top 60-100 feet of water, you'll soon start learning what the fish look like, which makes them easier to catch.

The last two seasons my troll rods have rarely been out of the rod storage lockers. Trolling to find fish for me is more of an early season technique for June, July, and part of August. But the late season has now transitioned into locating fish by using current reports, or running to areas that are known to produce, and on the run out, watching for the obvious signs such as birds working the surface. Once I'm in an area I believe should have fish, I use my sonar to find them. Starting in August and on into the fall, many times you'll see them jumping. If that's not an obvious sign, nothing will be!

On one trip in September, shortly after I upgraded my equipment, I was headed offshore with what seemed like the whole

Ilwaco fleet. I rarely ever leave the dock before 7 a.m. when running for tuna, but that particular morning we had a nice ocean, which allowed me to cruise at 40 knots. It wasn't long before I was catching and passing boats on the run out and after a 50-mile run, I came upon a parade of boats and anglers who had obviously heard the same report I had. Now I was faced with the question of where to start fishing. I really preferred not to be in the middle of all the boats so I moved off to the outer edge of where the bulk of the fleet was fishing. I had been listening to the radio chatter while making my way offshore and the people trolling were struggling to catch fish. When I finally pulled the throttles back and settled into the water, I saw what the problem was. The fish were on the sonar but they were scattered and were 30-50 feet deep. Once the water temperatures get into the mid-60s, generally late August and on into the fall, the tuna will stay a little deeper in the cooler water. There was a thermocline at about 40 feet and the tuna were scattered in and below that temperature variance. Tuna that deep rarely come up for troll gear making it difficult for those weaving back and forth on the ocean. A lot of boat traffic such as we had that day will also drive them down and keep them down until most of the boats leave the area.

You have two choices when faced with this scenario. You can either go find your own school of fish somewhere without all the boat pressure and hope the fish will be eager to bite troll gear, or you can learn how to go down after the fish and bring them up.

In our situation, I never pulled the troll rods out of the rod lockers but instead, instructed one person to drop some iron while another person pitched a swimbait and put it in the rod holder to drift. At the same time, another person threw chum and also put out a rod with live bait. When the fish are down in that zone, you have to go down and bring them up, and the combination of iron, swimbaits, and chum soon brought them right up under the boat. I had two to three people working iron, two others fishing live bait, and a couple of swimbait rods in rod holders with swimbaits drifting along. The bite was never wide open. One moment we would have three to four fish on and at times nothing, but we continued using the same technique as long as we had fish on the sonar and after three hours, we had a boat full of tuna.

Time after time we'd see a boat troll past us, frustrated at not catching fish, but continuing to troll. Knowing the fish were under the boat made it an easy decision as to what technique to use. Remember, finding them is half the equation and figuring out how to catch them is the other half. In this case we'd found them with the sonar, which also indicated to us we would need to go down and bring them up. This scenario has played out on my boat time and time again. An ocean full of boats and a reliable report confirmed there were definitely fish there which made it easy to just stop and look. At the end of the day, many frustrated anglers made their way back to port with little to show for their efforts because they chose to troll all day or didn't know how to fish using other techniques. A good sonar, properly adjusted, makes it much easier to find tuna and can help with the decision of what technique to use to catch them.

A recent survey on one of the local chat forums showed that less than 50% of anglers use their electronics/sonar to find tuna. Why wouldn't you want to use this effective method to help locate this fish?

Sonar has become something I use on a regular basis. During the late season, I may run for 40–50 miles with not much indication of tuna, only to get to my intended location, pull the throttles back, and find them waiting for me, but down 30–50 feet. I ring the dinner bell and we go to work.

And what do you do when the ocean has been rough for a week and there are no recent reports or worse yet, the web-based sea surface temperature service that you use doesn't have an update? You go back to where you've caught fish on previous trips. Hopefully you've saved those locations as waypoints. If you look at my chartplotter, you'll find it has many waypoints in tight clusters over the offshore canyons.

What Do They Eat?

ALBACORE ARE TOP CARNIVORES, PREYING ON SCHOOLING STOCKS such as anchovy and squid. They love clean blue water but they also love to eat, and in many cases you'll find them in clean green water where there's more food. They eat an enormous amount of food to fuel their high metabolism. These fish are feeding machines—they typically eat 5% of their body weight per day and at times can go on a feeding frenzy consuming as much as 25% of their body weight in 24 hours.

That may not sound like much, but if a 200-pound man ate 5% of his weight in a day, that would equal 10 pounds of food. It's a lot but it takes a lot to keep tuna fueled up since they are constantly moving as they coast down, deep into the water and swim back up. Sometimes they coast down as much as 3,200 feet deep and pretty much eat anything along the way. Also, they do not have a bladder, which requires them to be constantly swimming just to keep oxygenated water coming through their gills.

The phrase "match the hatch" is just as important in albacore fishing as it is to a fly fisherman pursuing trout in a stream. Your best success will generally come when you try to replicate what the tuna are feeding on. One of the best ways to determine that is to place a washdown hose in the mouth of the first tuna you land and see what gets flushed back out on the deck.

According to Oregon State University Marine Sciences, the top five items normally found in an albacore's belly off the Oregon and Washington coast are midwater shrimp, blue lanternfish, squid, saury, and anchovy.

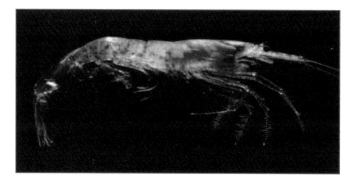

Midwater Shrimp

Midwater shrimp live at depths of 2,287 to 3,281 feet, or the "midwater," as it's called in the ocean, and migrate up and down the vertical water column. They are the most abundant crustaceans in the midwater which accounts for their appearance in the albacore's diet. They grow to 1.5 inches and have translucent red and white bodies but can take on a blue appearance from the dim light above.

A staple of the commercial troll fishery is the tuna clone in a squid shape. Squid are also commercially harvested for human consumption.

Squid

Saury

Cousin to the flying fish, the Pacific saury is a highly migratory species. Adults are generally found offshore, near the surface of the ocean, in schools. Juveniles associate with drifting seaweed.

Blue Lanternfish

Lanternfish account for as much as 65% of all deep-sea fish biomass. Lanternfish are generally small fish, ranging from about 0.79 to 11.81 inches in length, with most being under 6 inches. Shallow-living species are an iridescent blue to green or silver, while deeper-living species are dark brown to black. It is the most populous fish species in the open ocean.

Anchovy

California anchovy, also known as northern anchovy, ranges from Baja to British Columbia. They average 3–4 inches and are commonly used as live bait when fishing for tuna.

Juvenile Rockfish

The albacore diet is slightly different for anglers targeting tuna off the northern California coast. Here, the five most common food items found in the albacore belly are juvenile rockfish, krill, squid, saury, and anchovy.

Juvenile rockfish are found from southeast Alaska to Baja California and when found in the diet of albacore are juveniles of the many different species of rockfish that inhabit the waters from barely below the surface to the deep depths at the edge of the continental shelf.

Krill

The krill averages only about 2 inches in length, but it represents a giant-sized link in the global food chain. These small, shrimp-like crustaceans are essentially the fuel that runs the engine of the earth's marine ecosystems.

Krill feed on phytoplankton—microscopic, single-celled plants that drift near the ocean's surface and live off carbon dioxide and the sun's rays. Krill, in turn, are the main staple in the diets of liter-ally hundreds of different animals, from fish, to birds, to whales.

Gear

Trolling Rods - Trolling is how most of us started out. To troll you'll need good stout rods with reels that can handle the blistering runs that happen a lot in this fishery. The length of a trolling rod is not as important as the action of the rod. Traditionally most troll rods used for trolling clones and traditional gear will be 5'6"-6'6" in the 20 to 40-pound class. The key to a good troll rod is that it has a fairly stiff tip. Rods with a fast or soft tip will allow lures to skip too much on sporty days or days with a lot of wind chop, causing the lure not to stay down and run through the water properly.

Many times a rod that could be used for halibut or sturgeon fishing will also work fine for albacore. Some anglers prefer a short rod, at 5'6", in the back corners, and a longer rod ahead of it to keep the lines from crossing when making turns or during multiple hookups. Rods with roller guides are a bit of overkill for albacore but it gives you the flexibility to use the rod for other fisheries. A slotted rod butt also known as a gimbal butt is also something that can be useful but is not needed for these fish. If you use rods with gimbal butts, I'd recommend using a small, inexpensive fighting belt to pad your pelvis area. Continued use over time can weaken and tear the muscles in that area leading to a potential hernia eventually. After many years of fighting fish without one, I can tell you the cost of a $25 fighting belt is considerably cheaper than a $10,000 hernia surgery and the three months of recuperation that follows. I never realized stuffing a rod butt into my groin area would rub and wear on the muscles like it did. If you only fish a few times per year, it may not be as big of an issue.

I like rods with gimbal butts because they keep the rod upright and make it easier to handle, and when you pull the rod out of the rod holder, it will already be upright.

Troll rods used for soft plastic 3 to 5-inch shad-style-looking lures such as swimbaits can be just about any type of rod that can handle landing an albacore. A good stout salmon rod will work just fine. Most of the time you troll swimbaits at a much slower speed and they are not subject to hard jolts or skipping out of the water due to the trolling speed or any wind chop. I sometimes even use an eight-foot spin rod to troll a swimbait—the same rod I would use to cast that swimbait.

Trolling Reels - Reels have evolved a lot and although the big, bulky reels your father used will still work, the new kid on the block is smaller, more compact, more powerful, and weighs a third of what reels even five years ago weighed. They handle the fish easier and make it a shorter battle, allowing you to catch more fish on each outing.

The key to a good troll reel is that it's able to hold 300 yards of 40 to 65-pound line and it has a good, smooth drag system for those blistering runs. You'll generally spend about $180 or more for a good quality reel. In most cases, if you go cheap, you'll be back buying another reel after the first trip.

A two-speed reel is not needed for albacore but the cost difference between a single speed and a two-speed is generally not much more than $20 to $40. Also, the weight difference of only a couple ounces makes it an easy decision if you ever think you might want to use it for something else where a two-speed could come in handy.

I would stay away from using a reel with a line guide for trolling as very few reels on the market have a line guide that can handle the speed of line coming off the reel when hooking a fish on the troll and most will destroy the gearing in the line guide.

There are a lot of good quality reel manufacturers. I have enjoyed a Pro Staff relationship with Daiwa for many years and prefer the Saltist, Saltiga, and Lexa series of reels for albacore. If you're

Daiwa Saltist Lever Drag 2-Speed STTLD40-2SPD

looking for a reel that can cast a swimbait a mile and is available left- or right-handed, the Daiwa Lexa 400 is a great choice. I use and prefer the Daiwa Saltist Lever Drag 2-Speed STTLD40-2SPD on my troll rods.

That first trip offshore for me, fishing for tuna, was a real eye-opener; I was not prepared for what was about to happen. I was ill equipped for these muscled up sports cars of the deep and the very first fish took line off the reel at such a blistering speed that the line guide was a blur going side to side before things started coming apart. I could hear the gearing and drag system disintegrating in my hands. I was using heavy duty salmon reels but they are definitely no match for use as troll reels.

Good quality salmon reels such as a Daiwa Saltist reel with nice drags, will work for trolling swimbaits, working the iron, or fishing live bait because tuna don't make the same blistering runs when fishing these other methods.

A typical drag setting for albacore would be 7–12 pounds. Doesn't sound like much, does it? But just adjust a reel to 12 pounds and try to pull the line off the reel. It will surprise you just how strong that is. We start with 25 pounds of drag with the drag lever set in the strike position when I fish bluefin tuna on the East Coast. That's enough drag for the fish to pull you overboard if you're not braced or properly set. On one occasion, the boat was dead in the water and we were throwing chunks of chum overboard (chunking) for bluefin and had three rods go off at the same time. Try doing the dance with 100 to 300-pound tuna going all different directions. We'd back off the drags to about 12–15 pounds, allowing us

THE DARK SIDE

to follow our fish, then push the drag lever back to 25 pounds in the strike position once we had lines and fish separated.

An easy way to adjust the drag is using a small fish scale attached to the swivel, then put the rod in a rod holder pulling down on the line the same way a fish would be pulling line off the rod. The rule of thumb for drag settings is they should be no more than one third the breaking strength of the line you're using.

Line - You have a lot of good choices for line, whether using braid or monofilament . On my trolling reels, I spool them up with a minimum of 300 yards of 65-pound TUF-Line XP. The smaller line diameter of braid lets you get plenty of line on a reel allowing you to use a smaller, more compact reel. I then use a Double Albright knot (sometimes called Improved Albright) to attach various lengths up to 75 feet, of a 50-pound high vis (visibility) colored length of monofilament commonly referred to as a topshot because it's at the top of the spool of line on the reel.

The use of a Bimini Twist knot with a wind on topshot is another way to do the same thing. There are two reasons I use a monofila-ment topshot. One, it serves as a shock absorber since braid has no stretch and monofilament will stretch fairly well, absorbing some of the initial impact of a fish hitting a lure. Two, each topshot is

DEL STEPHENS

a different length on each rod, designating which rod holder it is assigned to for the day and where that lure goes in the spread pattern behind the boat.

Each rod has a number written on the underside of the reel seat. That number is the length of the topshot and a person only has to let the line out to the connection between the braid and the monofilament which helps them to know how far back their lure is trailing. Some guys will tie a knot or place a small piece of colored tape on the line at various lengths to do the same thing. When fishing with people who aren't as familiar with your boat, it helps them to remember where the rod goes after each fish is caught. It allows you the ability to get lines back out quickly and not worry about where to stop, when all you have to do is look for the connection. That may not sound like a difficult task, but when pandemonium strikes and you have multiple rods going off with triples and quads, people sometimes get in a daze and pretty soon they're just standing there with a blank look. It may sound strange, but they might even forget who they are, what their name is or even worse, where things need to be once everything settles down.

Some days the bite will come on but only last a short time while other days it might last all day. On the days when it never settles down, you need all the help you can get with a novice crew. The key to loading the boat up with fish is keeping things simple and being ready to capitalize on your opportunities. Having one or two lines in the boat with tuna flopping around while celebrating and exchanging high fives instead of getting those lines back out behind the boat as quickly as possible might mean the difference between a good day and a great day. Save those celebrations for when the gear is back in the water working.

I use Berkley Big Game High Vis line for my topshots, making it easy to see and and easy to follow the fish. The Big Game series is one of the most abrasion resistant lines I have ever used and when you have three engines hanging off the back, there's plenty to get tangled up in.

Swivels - At the end of the monofilament topshot is the place to attach a good test rated swivel that you can attach your lure to. If you have the misfortune of a bad tangle or worse, breaking off the topshot, you can tie the swivel onto the braid until you get a chance to redo the monofilament topshot. I would recommend backing off

the drag slightly so you don't snap something off on a hard strike.

It really doesn't matter what you use for a swivel as long as it's of good quality and preferably test rated. This is the link between your line and your leader and your success or failure could be determined by this small but critical item. If you go cheap, the fish will just tear it apart on the strike. I use a corkscrew swivel because it's tough and it's also quick to change lures out if needed.

Leaders - Trolling leaders on most lures such as clones or cedar plugs can be rigged with 4 to 6 feet of monofilament. There is no need to use fluorocarbon on your clones. I rig my 6-inch clones with 150 to 200-pound monofilament which makes it easy to just grab the leader and swing the fish over the rail versus taking the time to gaff it. The heavier leaders hold up a little better to abrasion and make it much easier to coil for storage at the end of the day. Lures that are 3 to 4 inches in length sometimes don't have an opening large enough for the large diameter of 200-pound test and in that situation, I rig them with 80-pound test. These leaders need to be

checked a little more frequently as they will chafe or wear more easily and should be re-rigged periodically. At the top of my leader I will crimp a good quality barrel swivel which makes it easier to change lures when needed.

Hooks - The size and style of hook to use really varies among anglers and they all have good reasons for how they like to rig them.

When I first started out, I had commercially rigged lures with heavy leaders attached to 10/0 double barbed hooks. That's what most of the commercial anglers used so it made perfect sense that I probably needed to use the same thing. A lot of the things I did early on in my tuna education were based on what the commercial anglers were doing or using. There's nothing wrong with that, but they're running a different type of system with fixed lines much like a handline would be for us, and they're also fishing for a living. It's important for them that when multiple fish hit, that the fish all stay attached considering the anglers rarely ever stop the boat when trolling. They're typically using much heavier gear to hold up to all the hard strikes.

I quickly learned that the tuna hit these lures like a freight train going the opposite direction at Mach 3. They bury the double hooks, at times making them difficult to remove, which takes up valuable fishing time while you struggle to unhook them. I then progressed to using barbless double hooks and that made life easier. It's not a bad way to go for a sport person, but you'll periodically lose a fish if you just let them hang without much tension on them, such as when you have more fish hooked than people to reel them in. In this case, you might want to keep the boat in gear at an idle speed until someone can get to all the rods.

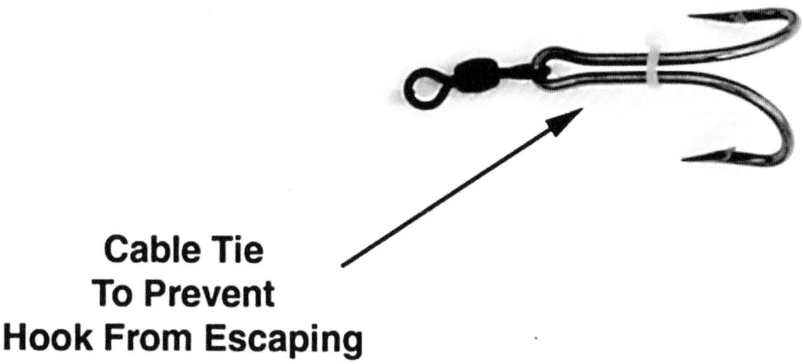

**Cable Tie
To Prevent
Hook From Escaping**

10/0 Southern Tuna Style Hook

A good setup using barbless double hooks is to attach a barrel swivel to the hook end of the leader and prior to fishing that day, attach the barbless hook, threading it onto the swivel. If you're worried about it coming off while fishing or while battling a fish, you can also put a small zip tie around the shanks of the hook just down from the swivel. At the end of the day, cut the zip tie and now you can roll your leaders up without the worry of tangling hooks.

I like to use a single 8/0 to 10/0 southern style barbed tuna hook on my 5 to 6-inch trolling lures and scale down to a single 5/0 hook on the smaller, 3 to 4-inch trolling lures.

Handlines - The oldest known fishing method is the handline, or meat line as some people refer to it. The basic form and techniques used back in the early days of mankind haven't changed much over the millennia. Also referred to as blue cord, handlines can be made inexpensively and are a very effective method for catching tuna. They are very common on commercial boats and are used occasionally by sport anglers. It's not uncommon for sport boats to use a couple of handlines along with their rod and reel setups. They are trolled at the same speed as the lures on rods. They don't provide the glamour or excitement of line singing off a reel at a blistering speed, but are very effective if you're just interested in meat fishing.

A typical handline setup consists of a length of 400-pound test braided nylon. Lengths used on sport boats can be as short as 20 feet and as long as 100 feet and will have a heavy duty rubber bungee rigged as a shock absorber on the end that attaches to the boat. The other end has a high quality 250-pound test or greater rated swivel. To that you attach the lure you wish to run behind it and it should have a minimum 200-pound test leader. The only give in this whole setup is the bungee and a good hard strike can still destroy things.

When deploying a handline, be sure to attach it to something very secure such as a cleat, or you may be sadly dissapointed when a tuna hits and tears the handline off the boat along with what it was attached to. If deployed out behind the boat with only a lure attached, the lure will run on the surface or slightly below. When a tuna strikes, the handline will typically go down. You don't have to stop or slow the boat although it's easier to pull the fish in if you do. Gloves would be prudent to keep from chafing or cutting your hands. Due to the lack of a drag system on a reel, your back and arms become the drag. To avoid a tangled mess on the deck of the boat, when pulling the cord in, it's helpful to have a container such as a small rectangular laundry basket, sitting in the corner on the floor, to coil the cord down into as it's being pulled in.

A good way to fish the handline at a deeper depth is to attach it to a diver and then attach the lure to the diver or use a release clip attached to the diver. When a tuna strikes the lure, the line pops free and you don't have to deal with the blue cord or diver until it's time to redeploy. I've also seen guys use a short section of logging chain (about 1–2 feet long) at the lure end of the handline where they then attach a swivel to have a method of attaching the lure. The logging chain gives the handline weight to take it down under the surface and it also causes a bubble trail when water flows through the links, helping to work as somewhat of a teaser.

Divers - There are times the tuna are down below the surface and some guys like to use divers or planer boards to go down after them. I have only used them a few times and prefer other methods for bringing the fish up. But there are others who swear by divers and planer boards and as I mentioned earlier, it's good to develop your own style of how you like to fish and get good at it. There are obviously many ways to catch these fish.

Salty planers (page 42) are a stainless steel diver with a piece of lead to help take it down. They come in various sizes and most have so much pull you'd either have to use a heavier rod/ reel combination or use the planers with a handline. Some just use a handline while others attach a release clip to the diver much like you would with a downrigger. The diver pulls straight whereas some planer boards actually work a little side to side like a feeding fish does at times.

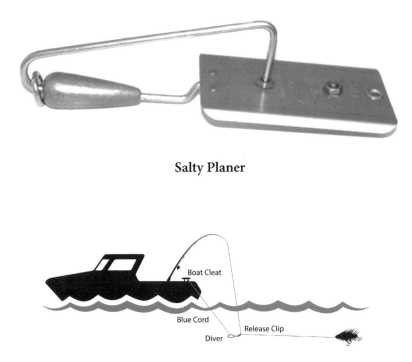

Salty Planer

Blue Cord with Diver and Release Clip

Jigs and Lures

CLONES - ONE OF THE MOST COMMON TROLLING LURES USED IS A clone. Clones are a favorite of commercial tuna anglers because they're tough and can handle being chewed on without getting torn up. They're designed to replicate squid and come in various colors and sizes. Typically made of a tough vinyl, each clone has a lead weight inside it, which helps keep it down in the water and running flat. Clones traditionally come in two lengths for albacore—3–4 inches or 5–6 inches.

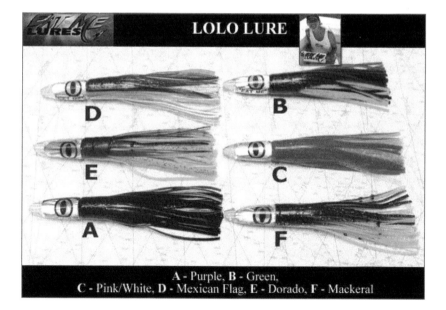

A - Purple, B - Green,
C - Pink/White, D - Mexican Flag, E - Dorado, F - Mackeral

Something to improve your odds when the bite gets a little tough is running a clone with a softer vinyl skirt which will cause it to puff up and down similar to a squid squirting along. A quick search on the internet will reveal a lot of variations to the tuna clone. Creating a different look coming through the water is what most anglers are after whether they're using a hex headed lure, a feathered lure, or a lure with a jetted head that creates a bubble trail for a hungry tuna to key in on.

A - Pink, B - Green/Yellow Pink Skirt, C - Purple/Black, D - Mexican Flag

DEL STEPHENS

Tuna Jets - A tuna jet looks like a clone, but has a metal head with multiple holes and when trolled, the water shooting through the holes creates a bubble trail. They come in various sizes, generally come in many of the same colors as other trolling lures, and are another option in your arsenal of what you can choose to pull behind the boat.

Cedar Plugs - Made from cedar and very popular, they look like a cigar with a lead head with a single hook on the trailing end. At times they come in painted colors but the unpainted cedar plug is the most popular. You troll them at the same speeds as the other artifical lures. They also work well during the late season when things sometimes get a little tough and the fish aren't biting as much. Trolling a purple/black cedar plug way back on the shot gun rig has been known to pick off a schoolie sized bluefin tuna running with albacore.

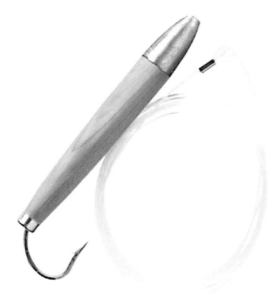

Diving Lures - At times, using something that can get subsurface can help bring fish up into your spread. Rapala X-Raps and Yo-Zuris Magnums are some of the most commonly used lures and can be very effective. They come in various sizes and I have not noticed much of a difference as to what gets bitten more, although the bigger lures tend to go deeper and there are days when that does make a difference. Some people take the treble hooks off and replace them with siwash hooks. I have not had much success with this as they tend to roll once in a while when rigged like this. I like to remove the belly hook and just leave the tail hook rigged the same as it came out of the box. They tend to hit the tail hook most of the time and you rarely miss a fish with the treble hooks. If you choose to leave both treble hooks just know they will catch everything inside the boat as well and are a pain to store, hooking and tangling with anything they even get close to. I have them in many different colors but prefer the sardine, bunker, and dark purple colors.

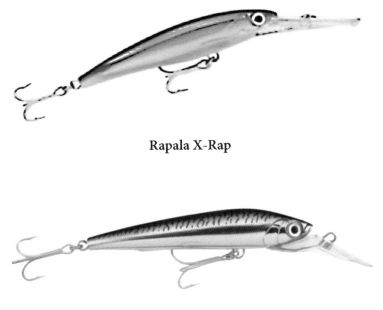

Rapala X-Rap

Yo-Zuri Magnum

Williamson Speed Pro Deep

The Speed Pro Deep has an auto tuning feature that keeps it running properly for better, consistent action. Some of the earlier Magnum Rapalas with the metal bill would need to be tuned after catching a fish, taking up time before being able to be re-deployed. The Speed Pro Deep's self aligning feature has eliminated that problem.

Daisy Chains - As the name implies, it's a chain of lures (page 48) on a heavy monofilament, such as 200-pound test. The lures are spaced evenly apart and at the end of the chain is a lure with a hook. The theory behind this is that the last lure is the slow poke or weak bait and the tuna will target the weak. Most of the time they're made with clones, but I've seen folks also use various other things such as 000 size spin glows with a clone at the end. The big spin glows really throw a spray and raise quite a ruckus. When made and used for albacore, they're typically about 6 feet long. If you were fishing big bluefin tuna, you'd probably be using daisy chains 10–12 feet long with 12-inch lures.

Pink Daisy Chain going through the water

DEL STEPHENS

TROLLING 101

FIRST THING OUT OF MY WIFE'S MOUTH WAS "TELL THEM TO forget about trolling." She seems to be enjoying her newfound success with working the iron; I haven't trolled much the last few years and I'll discuss why in later chapters.

Most people learning to fish for tuna start out learning how to troll. It's the most common method used to catch tuna of all species and it's also how I started.

When trolling for tuna, you want to create an attractive scenario for the fish below that will bring them up behind your boat to eat. In this situation, the dark massive shadow of the bottom of your boat should appear to be a bait ball that is under attack and getting pushed along by predator fish. Behind it are your lures which appear to be bait fish or squid that have been separated from the safety of the bait ball but are trying to get back to it so they will not be eaten. The tuna below sees this attractive opportunity and raise up to feed, exploding on your lures and peeling line off your reels so that you can now battle those fish to the boat and over the rail. And that is what captivates so many tuna anglers. We spend a lot of money, countless hours in preparation, and travel very long distances offshore, all to hear those reel drags singing when the strongest pelagic fish in the ocean are fooled by your presentation of a trolling spread.

Early in the season, trolling squid-like clones is a very effective way to locate and catch tuna. Later in the season, the troll bite will taper off and you have to resort to other techniques for catching and finding these fish.

Trolling is one of the oldest methods used to find fish and everyone can do it. Like anything else, how good you get depends on how much time and effort you put into learning the finer details. And as I mentioned before, there's a saying in the Northwest that anyone can catch a tuna in July, and it's pretty much true. Just run offshore, deploy the gear, and start catching tuna. Once you find the tuna or you've seen signs that indicate you're in an area that should have tuna, it's time to deploy the gear.

It's mind-boggling how many styles of lures are out there that will catch albacore and over the last 20 years, I think I've tried most of them. I've refined it down to what I prefer to use, but in an effort to cover most of the most common lures that are available, I'll try to show and explain the ones that most people use. The biggest thing to keep in mind is—it's more important how you fish a lure than what lure you're fishing. Don't get me wrong, the lure you fish is important, but how you put out your spread and where you position your lures in the spread are integral aspects of having a successful day on the water. This is also where you as an angler start to develop your own style of how you fish and what works for you. The success or failure of what you do as an angler is vital to becoming confident in what you're doing.

If you've ever been out there trolling, listening to the radio chatter, and heard that one boat is clobbering the fish while you're just picking off a fish here and there, it's most likely the little things that are making a difference. I've been in that position. I was fishing within 100 yards of a buddy boat who was trolling Mexican Flag colored SevenStrand tuna clones. He was getting doubles, triples, and quads while I was just lucky to get bitten at all while trolling the identical lures. I switched out to another color, but still the same style of lures, and suddenly it was game on. We soon plugged the boat and it really begged the question of what was the difference between his boat and setup versus my boat and setup. They were both 26-foot Stripers, and the only difference was that he had twin outboards versus my single I/O outdrive.

It wasn't until later that we realized that he had been trolling in a different direction and when we made the switch from one color to the other, we also happened to change the direction we were trolling. Sometimes it doesn't matter, but many days the direction you're trolling—whether going east to west or north to south and vice versa—will make a difference. This is one of those little things that can mean the difference between a so-so day and a great day. On sporty days you may not have much of a choice. If the wind and waves are coming out of the west, chances are that trolling into them won't be as productive because your jigs are going to be popping out of the water and the boat ride is also probably going to be very uncomfortable. In some situations, you just have to turn with the wind and waves and troll with it.

Inboard boats traditionally have the cleanest prop wash, which allows you to run your jigs in close off the stern and longer off the side rods. In some cases, dual-prop pod drives and triple outboard engines can create turbulence coming off the center of the transom, and it sometimes helps to put your jigs farther back when deploying the stern rods, keeping the side or outrigger rods in closer. On the run out, I usually trim the boat and motors for the best ride and efficiency, but once I slow down and start to troll, I raise my trim tabs up all the way, then lower all my motors to full down. I come up to troll speed and look back at how clean the water is coming off my prop wash. I will play with the trim tabs and motor trim until I get a clean prop wash with as little turbulence coming off the boat and motors as possible.

Boat attitude is another one of those little things that can make a difference. I'm not talking about people's attitude onboard. I'm talking about how a boat goes through the water and in turn, how water comes off the boat. It makes a difference, although that's not something you can change very easily, if at all.

Big single or twin screws on a boat can create harmonics that often work well to raise fish. On numerous occasions I've seen big boats with twin screws that would raise fish when everyone around them struggled to get bitten. Commercial fishermen stay very in tune with what RPMs their engines are turning to create the best harmonics for their boat and in turn, the best scenario for raising and catching tuna.

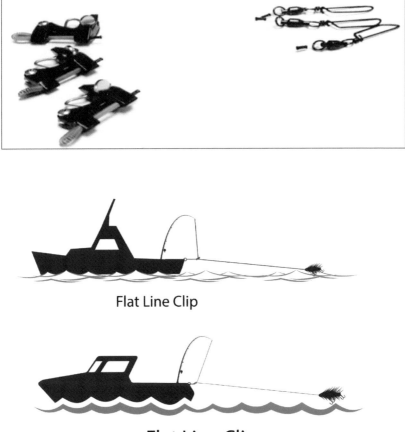

Flat Line Clip

Flat Line Clip

Another issue to watch for is jigs skipping through the surface on days when there is wind chop or large swells. Ideally, you want them coming through the water without jumping or skipping. If your jigs are skipping through the surface, attach a release clip to the line to lower the entry into the water, causing it to run under the surface more. When I run my jigs within 20 to 25 feet off the transsom, I always place them in release clips, also known as flat line clips. I like to attach the release clip to a cleat low on the back of the boat. When I'm done fishing, I take them off the cleat and store them until the next time. Some guys will mount them permanently on the outer edge at the top of the transom. You see this more often on big sportfishers.

In Oregon you can fish with as many rods as you can handle. The key to making this work effectively is to make sure you have your fishing lines and jigs spread out so they don't tangle when making turns or when you have multiple fish hooked up on all the rods and now they are going in various directions before you can get to them. I like to deploy my lures or jigs sometimes as close as 25 feet from the transom to the longest jigs back about 65 feet, and never more than 15 feet apart. Which means if I'm fishing with the shortest jigs in close behind the boat, it's not that far back to the longest jigs. Keeping your spread somewhat tight and close together will get you more multiple hookups. Some anglers like to fish farther back such as 65 feet on their short rods and way out around 100 to 120 feet on the long rods. In either situation, I still like to keep the spread close together. I tend to get more hookups fishing my spread closer to the boat, but things can change out there and if my longest rods were getting bitten but nothing was happening in close, I'd want to move my whole spread back a little to put more of my lures in the strike zone. The same would be applicable if the strikes were coming on the short rods. You'd want to bring the spread in closer to capitalize on this.

If you've ever read articles in magazines that talk about putting your lure on the backside of the second, third, fourth, or fifth wake, keep in mind that in most cases, they're referring to big sportfishers. The distance behind a boat to the fourth, fifth, or sixth wake really varies between boats, especially when you're considering boats 26 feet up to 60 feet. Every boat, depending on its size and prop system, throws a different wake pattern. It really doesn't matter what wake you're on, it's more important to have the jig running in smooth, clean water, which is either on top of the wake or on the backside and not popping or jumping out of the water. You do not want the jig running in the trough in front of it.

Most anglers use a V- or W-shaped pattern when they deploy their gear. Using a rod down the middle and way back is known as the shotgun rig, and many times it will be attached to a center rigger or on small boats, the rod might be placed in the rocket launcher up overhead.

Trolling speed for most lures such as clones or cedar plugs will be somewhere around 4 to 8 knots but don't worry about how fast that is in miles per hour because at these slower speeds, it's pretty much about the same speed. I mention this because I get asked that question frequently during my seminars. Play with your troll speed to find what works best for your boat. Some anglers make note of how many RPMs their engines are running when their jigs are coming through the water the best. Adjust your speed to how your lures are coming through the water to get the best presentation. You want them in the water and not skipping along. On sporty days you might need to go a little slower just to keep them in the water.

Have you ever heard someone say, "Man, I never should've sold that boat. That boat caught fish!" That's actually more true than people realize. Some boats are very "fishy." Two really big factors can influence this—how the water is coming off the boat and too much voltage being discharged into the water. As mentioned earlier, there's often not much you can do about how the water comes off your boat, but you can usually address the voltage being discharged. Too much voltage coming off a boat can be a real deal killer when fishing saltwater. It doesn't matter what species you're fishing. If you're fishing fairly close to your boat, such as with tuna or salmon, too much voltage will push them back.

I had an instance one summer which caused me to struggle catching salmon during the Columbia River Buoy 10 fishery. I put the boat into my slip for the summer in mid-July but due to a busy schedule getting the Deep Canyon Challenge Tuna Tournament ready, I never had an opportunity to take it out and fish prior to the tournament. I then fished the tournament on the boat of one of my crew members. A few days later, I made it down to my boat to do some fishing only to find all four batteries were completely dead and the onboard charger switch was in the "Off" position. The remainder of that day was spent replacing batteries and the next five days, fishing with family members. I have grown accustomed to getting my fair share of salmon when fishing this fishery but had noticed on a few occasions when boats around us were in a hot bite, that we didn't seem to be getting our share of them. Later that week, I noticed the breaker was tripping after we plugged the shore power cord into the boat. This prompted me to take a day off from fishing to have the boat checked and I was not surprised when the tech mentioned the onboard charger had shorted out and was discharging voltage into the water. He replaced the charger and our bite imediately rose back up to what I was used to.

Most every boat puts off some level of voltage, so make sure to check your zinc anodes regularly, making sure they're in good shape. You can also check your voltage, but I would recommend turning all the same electronics on that you would normally have on while fishing, and then check it. Ideally, you'd like to have a positive voltage of 0.5 to 0.7 volts. Anything over that can have a negative effect on your fishing. If it's above that, check your zincs and if they're in good shape, you might have a short somewhere. If you change any of the electronics, check your voltage.

Now that we've talked about the boat issues and how to avoid things that can shoot you in the foot, let's get the gear out and get on with fishing! We have the boat set up and we're offshore in an area we think might have fish—it's time to start putting the gear overboard. One little item to remember is to make sure you have the reel clickers turned on. If you don't, you might miss a strike, and trolling even a mere 15 to 20 seconds after the hookup, a tuna can dump 300 yards off a reel in the blink of an eye. This really gets your attention if suddenly you hear what sounds like a gunshot, signaling that the tuna has taken everything—ripping your line, rod, and reel from your boat. Either the line breaks or the rod does, depending on which was the weakest link. These fish are built for speed, and the power in even a 20-pound fish is amazing. They will definitely test your gear, letting you know immediately if you came to play underequipped.

Nothing will get your adrenaline pumping quicker than when the first reel starts singing, but don't pull the throttles back just yet. Keep the boat moving forward another 7 to 10 seconds and you'll increase your chances of doubles, quads, and loading up all the rods. Also, this is where some folks believe you'll be more efficient and get more multiple hookups when all the lures are the same color and same weight. Try it.

Don't even attempt to take the rod out of the holder or think you can do anything to stop them from running while the boat is still moving forward. Just stand there and listen to the music of the clickers singing and once the boat stops you can proceed to bring the fish in. As you bring the fish in, you might want to turn the clicker off or you're going to be labeled a rookie as no one wants to listen to it as you reel.

If you're using outriggers or have multiple lines out, whether hooked up or not, and the wind is blowing, be careful allowing the boat to drift back or off to the side as this can lead to a tangled mess. If you have more lines hooked up than anglers, that's not a bad problem to have. Someone just needs to keep the other fish tight while someone else is bumping the boat in and out of gear just enough to keep things straight.

A good way to add to the count at the end of the day is to deploy a drop back rig as soon as the first rod starts singing. A drop back rig is a rod with a lure such as a swimbait or possible iron that is tossed out the back of the boat at the first sound of a hookup. You can't be standing around with your thumb in your ear when the rod goes off or you'll miss the chance. If you have to reach up into a rocket launcher for a rod or hunt for it— forget it. You missed your chance.

A few years back I had the opportunity to fish with a buddy on his boat. I brought a drop back rig but his boat only had enough gunnel rod holders for the rods being used during trolling. It left no place to lean a rod for quick access and the only extra rod holders were up in the rocket launchers, forcing me to lean the rod up in the corner of the cockpit. One of his crew members felt a need to keep the cockpit neat and orderly and the first couple of times that I went to grab the rod it was gone, as the crew member had put it up overhead in a rocket launcher. It took a little threatening to beat him with the fish whacker and a couple of hookups for him to see why I wanted it close by. He quickly learned and was on it every time after that. We landed over 40 fish that day and 8 to 10 of them came from the drop back rig.

When the troll rod goes off, you only have about 3 to 5 seconds to pitch the drop back rig out the back. Don't toss it out in some other direction—it should go in the direction of the hooked fish, allowing it to free spool while the boat is still moving ahead trying to load up the other troll rods. Generally, you'll feel the fish when it picks up the lure. A lot of times it will just feel like a trout bit the lure and you only have to engage the drag. If it doesn't hook a fish by the time the boat stops to reel in the troll-caught fish, just flip the bail or set the drag and put it in a rod holder while you're bringing in the hooked fish. Many times the bobbing action of the boat will work the lure and entice a strike.

OUTRIGGERS

PEOPLE NEW TO TUNA FISHING OFTEN ASK IF THEY REALLY NEED outriggers to catch albacore. The simple answer is no. If you plan to fish other species of tuna, outriggers can provide some advantages. For many years I fished albacore without them. Then I went through the phase where I thought I needed them and I bought a pair of 18-foot Taco Outriggers. I installed a pair of Taco Grand Slam mounts to the hard top of my 26-foot Striper and thought I had it made. But the 18-foot length was too long for the 26-foot boat and when running in sporty seas, the outriggers would whip wildly and it was not uncommon for one of them to come crashing down. Things making crashing sounds while running on a rough ocean are not what you want to hear and will definitely put you on edge. I would not recommend outriggers longer than 15 feet for boats less than 30 feet, especially if they're mounted on the hard top. My current boat is 33 feet and came with 15-foot Taco Outriggers which rarely get used.

Outriggers definitely make a boat look sexy and provide the advantage of spreading your lures out over a larger area. They can also put your lures out in the quieter water beside the boat.

Outriggers are commonly made out of aluminum, fiberglass, or carbon fiber. They come in one piece or collapsible configurations. Lightweight anodized aluminum and fiberglass options are generally the less expensive path while carbon fiber is the more expensive route. The longer ones made for big boats will typically have spars scattered throughout their length to provide more rigidity and strength. The longer, one-piece riggers are almost always mounted on the side of the wheelhouse or flybridge where they'll ride without too much trouble, although many of them will not go very low to the side, which can be a problem on windy days. Outriggers travel better in the upright, locked position and when you arrive at your intended fishing location, you should adjust down to where they're at a 30-45 degree angle from the top of the boat. On small boats, that might look like the outrigger is slightly higher above level. They just need to be high enough so they don't dip and touch the water from the side to side rocking of the boat as it travels through the water. This lower position will help keep your lures traveling through the water better, drawing more strikes versus skipping on the surface out of the water part of the time when raised higher off the water. If the wind is blowing much over 12 to 15 knots, you'll experience lines crossing and could end up with a tangled mess from time to time. Using outriggers during windy conditions requires someone to be constantly paying attention to where the lines are and in most cases, requires some adjustment as to how far back the lures are, in order to prevent tangles. Tangles or a lure spread that's not efficient are a waste of time.

Taco, Lee, Tigress, and Rupp are some of the most popular manufacturers of aluminum outriggers and they make them in varying lengths and styles depending on the size and configuration of the boat. They are made from anodized aluminum and typically have eyelets evenly spaced the length of the rigger. Aluminum outriggers with eyelets allow you to run more than one lure from each outrigger. A halyard or line is strung through the eyelets and back down to the boat where it goes through a small pulley attached to a bungee system to keep it snug. Halyards made of heavy 400-pound monofilament tend to go through the eyelets and the pulley on the bungee easier than braided nylon cord. The halyards also come in various colors making them easy to see, especially if you're running two halyards on one outrigger. You could rig one with a halyard that's black and another that's red to keep them easier to separate and adjust.

Where the two ends of the halyard come together, you attach an outrigger release clip. There are basically two types of releases, one with a roller and the other with a wire clip. There are varying styles of each and most are reliable and will work fine. I have used both types from various manufacturers and prefer the Nok-Outs made by Rupps. They are a roller style release that has a ball bearing at each end of the roller with a tension adjustment on both ends, allowing for a finer adjustment and a smooth release.

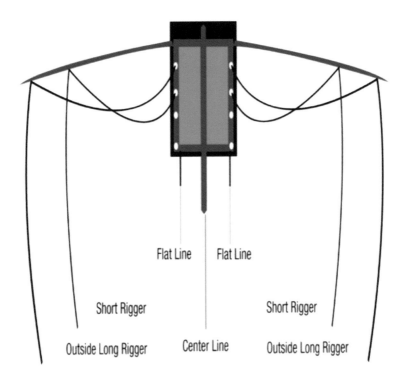

Flat Line   Flat Line

Short Rigger   Short Rigger

Outside Long Rigger   Center Line   Outside Long Rigger

I've seen anglers get pretty creative when it comes to ways to get their lures out away from the boat. I have a friend who sometimes uses his Cannon downriggers with the 5-foot booms swiveled out to the side. A great way to go, but you want to be very careful to use release clips adjusted carefully so as not to have a strike tear out the swivel locking mechanism or worse yet, bend the booms.

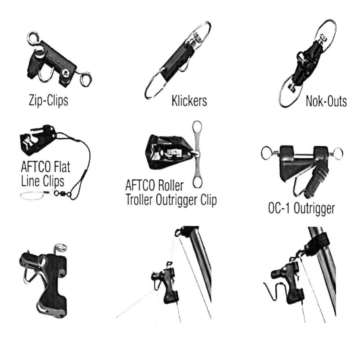

Zip-Clips

Klickers

Nok-Outs

AFTCO Flat Line Clips

AFTCO Roller Troller Outrigger Clip

OC-1 Outrigger

Flat line booms are also a viable option. They are generally about five feet in length, have a rod holder mounted on top, and fit down into the rod pocket. Another option similar to this is a rod holder with a gimbal end that fits down inside the rod pocket and can be turned to any direction. These two options also need to have a tether attached to the boat to prevent this type of rod holder from falling overboard when the rod is removed. When they don't have tension against them, they have a tendency to come out of the rod pocket as the rod is coming out and I've heard plenty of stories of folks losing them when they weren't somehow attached to the boat.

Teasers

A TEASER IS JUST WHAT THE NAME IMPLIES. IT'S A DEVICE THAT IS used to tease the fish up or into your lure spread and entice a bite. Teasers come in all shapes and configurations.

Spreader bars are a type of teaser and are very common in the northeast canyons off places like New Jersey and over time, they have started showing up in the spreads off Oregon and Washington. The versions used in places like the Hudson Canyon in the Northeast are typically made from high-grade metal with a 30 to 36-inch bar. The teasers have six-inch squid lined up on a string coming off the bar and some versions will have the centerline as the longest row ending with a squid rigged with a hook.

Early on in my tuna career, I spent well over $1,700 for a collection of these spreader bars and gave them a whirl. First thing I'll say—they do raise and catch fish. But the second thing is—they are a pain in the butt to handle on a small boat under 30 feet. You fight with them letting them out, hoping to not get them tangled, then they force you to retrieve them, just to untangle and let out again. Once you get them back out, you fiddle with them to make sure they're properly trailing with the bar just above the water. If the bar is not out of the water, the darn thing just cartwheels along and that's not teasing anything other than cuss words out of your mouth. I have learned to fish them effectively and they fish better when used on outriggers where the riggers can help keep them slightly elevated. Although when they get bitten or the bite kicks in and gets hot, they wind up in a heap on the deck of your boat tangled with your other gear, and now the cuss words are flowing again while you spend valuable time dealing with them instead of fishing.

My other pet peeve about these big bars is they can scratch the graphics on my boat.

A few years back, someone had a great idea to have a Salty Dog yard sale and these things were such a pain they went right to the top of my list when I started looking at what I thought I needed to part with. I sold them at bargain basement prices. It takes quite a bit for a tuna guy to want to part with anything they think might be of use so you can image how I felt about those spreader bars.

I used to keep a storage unit for all my tuna gear and just when I thought I had it thinned down to what I thought was really the most essential I decided to try chasing bluefin tuna in the Outer Banks of North Carolina.

Oh brother, here we go again. And of all things, guess what they were using for teasers? Yep. Here's where you question yourself and attempt a reality check. The last thing you want is for your friends to find out you sold something so valuable that now you need them again because you now have another addiction and of course, I spent another couple thousand dollars buying new spreader bars to replace the others.

I have no intention of fishing these bars for albacore, but every chance I get to chase big bluefin off our coast, they'll be onboard ready to deploy.

I do however, use smaller spreader bars for albacore. The bars are 10-16 inches wide and are made out of a softer plastic that doesn't scratch my boat. Yeah, I'm a little anal about scratching the graphics on the side of the boat. The smaller bars are much easier to deal with and even straighten themselves out most of the time. Lay them in the water and just let them out about 10 feet keeping the bar slightly above the water and in most cases if they're tangled, the water coming against the small squids will untangle them.

I fish the spreader bars off the long rigger but have a friend who likes to use them off the short rods in the back corners. Again, it comes down to your fishing style and what works for you.

I was fishing on a buddy's boat a few years back and we decided he would fish his style and technique off one side and I would fish my own style on the other side of the boat. We were each fishing three rods—one on the outrigger where I was running a small 12-inch spreader bar about 55 feet back, one inside of that about 35-40 feet back, and a corner rod which at times was barely 20 feet back. He had three rods scattered about the same distance as my side and each with only a single lure.

I was catching fish at a pretty good clip but only on my two inside shorter rods and the teaser was not getting hit. He was catching a fish here and there but not at the pace of my two rods. So he decided to put out a teaser using a small plastic bird teaser in line with his lure on the rod attached to his outrigger. The bite on his side improved slightly but not at the pace as my two short rods.

The lure on my spreader bar was not getting bitten so I decided to pull it in and take the teaser off. Bad mistake—because now my bite died on all the rods on my side of the boat. I put the teaser back on and back out where it had been and the bite picked right back up. Lesson learned—just because the teaser bar wasn't getting bitten, it was still teasing fish into the spread and was very effective at getting action on my other lures.

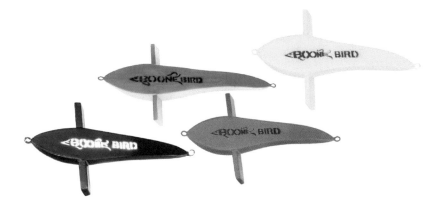

I've had days where the lure on the spreader bar was getting bitten but in some cases, that may not happen. Don't fret it if it's drawing fish to the other rods.

If you have riggers that allow you to run a short rigger, put the spreader bar on another rod or teaser reel and place it back in the spread just as a teaser. Now you can fish all your rods in their usual places and hopefully load them up with multiple hookups.

Colors

ONE OF THE MOST COMMON QUESTIONS I GET DURING MY SEMINARS has to do with trolling all the same colors. First thing I'll tell you is there's a lot of debate on this topic. And perhaps one factor in this debate is that the color of the lures can appear to change throughout the day or moon phase according to many commercial jig boat captains. Many anglers feel that dark colors, such as purple/black, have better contrast on cloudy or overcast days. Likewise lighter colors, such as pink/white, zucchini, all white, or pearl, work better on brighter days. In many cases, I've seen the day start out overcast or with dark clouds during the first part of the day, then slowly burn off, and by noon be a bluebird day with bright sunshine.

Should you put out all one color or mix it up? Some people subscribe to the theory that trolling all one color is more effective than mixing the colors up in your spread. Their belief is that if the lead fish in a school is given only one choice of color, if all lines are running identical lures, this should encourage multiple hookups as opposed to running multiple colors. They say one of the most important things you can do is not provide tuna a choice when it comes to the lures in the spread. They believe this one factor denies more anglers the opportunity for an epic day than anything else. There is a reason to run all the same lures in your spread. What is important is how they swim and where they swim. They want the same lure and the same weight. That's one theory.

Another theory is just the opposite—it's to give them a variety. Albacore are no different from any other predator and they will gravitate to what might look like the weakest looking—or different colored—lure in the spread. Then, if you get one to bite, in many cases it will incite the others to join in and load up all the rods.

In most situations, I like to put out all the same color, but I generally mix it up with the sizes and styles of lures. It's not uncommon for me to put out a small hex head, large hex head, small clone, large clone, and a small jet. If they start biting one particular lure, I'll put more of that kind of lure out.

One of the biggest things that influences this is developing your own style of how you like to fish based on what works for you. This confidence in what works for you is your best friend.

When I started out, I had a zillion colors and sizes of everything you could imagine but as the years have passed, I have fine-tuned what works for me. If it's dark or overcast in the morning there's a good chance I'm going to put out purple/black combinations to start. If I know I'm in an area that's holding fish but I don't get bitten, then I start changing things around.

If the day is bright or the overcast is light, I'm going to put out pink/white or zucchini combinations. Pink/white is probably the most common color lure that trails behind my boat. I have found and developed confidence in what works for me and when I put that lure overboard, I expect and believe it's going to catch fish.

Fishing Swimbaits

First experiences are hard to forget, especially if they're the kind that put you on a high for weeks. It's been many years since my first experience chasing tuna in my own boat, but I still remember it well. The high fives and exhilarating feelings at the end of those first few trips coming home with plugged fish boxes. The great white fisherman coming home from the sea, chest all pumped up and plenty to show for his efforts. Life couldn't be better. The bounty of the sea was all but jumping into the boat on its own without much effort. It was early July and we'd run offshore, threw out feathered tuna clones on the troll, and wham, fish on! It was doubles, triples, and an occasional quad. It was literally that easy. It almost didn't matter what color or size we put out there.

Then it happened—late season. We were 50 miles offshore on a very flat, greasy ocean the first time I heard the words "fish trap." It was late August and we had been whacking them regularly since early July that year. The forecast couldn't have been better and we were anxious to experience great fishing on a smooth, greasy, flat ocean. Tuna anglers long for flat days like that. The run out was quick and once we arrived at our intended destination, we wasted no time in deploying our troll gear. We saw other boats, so obviously we had found the fish, right?

The first hour went by with no strikes so we decided to move around looking for that fish willing to sacrifice its life so our egos could be salvaged. Another hour went by with no cooperation. Soon we had changed gear a few more times trying different combinations and colors before another hour passed with still nothing in the box. We'd see an occasional jumper but they didn't seem to want anything we had to offer. By now we had thrown pretty much everything in our tuna arsenal at them to no avail. I was still somewhat new to the tuna game and obviously had more to learn. Periodically I'd hear someone on the VHF radio talk about using a "fish trap" but could never get them to answer me after I'd call them on the radio.

It was a long, hot, frustrating day on the water and we came home with our tail between our legs and nothing to show for our efforts. For a beginning tuna guy who had been living the dream and walking on a cloud, this was the bottom of the bottom. Talk about taking the wind out of your sails! I felt like I had just gone 10 rounds with Mike Tyson—beaten, battered, and bruised—my ego was chopped back down to reality.

It took me a few days to find someone who could actually tell me what a fish trap was, only to learn it was not some type of trap but a soft plastic lure made from pouring liquid into a mold, letting it harden, and then popping it out. They were made by Fish Trap Lures in Southern California and I wasted no time in stocking up on numerous colors. The owner of Fish Trap Lures, Barry Brightenburg, was very generous with his knowledge and well versed on which colors and sizes should work best for albacore. My ego was still quite bruised, so I made sure I ordered enough to last a while. On my next trip offshore, I would be prepared. That last trip was burned well into my mind. I still remember it very clearly as if it were just yesterday.

Fish traps are commonly known as swimbaits today and there are a number of manufacturers making them. Big Hammer, located in Southern California, is the largest and is one of the main suppliers on the West Coast. Their website, www.swimbait.com, has examples of many colors and sizes to choose from.

Swimbaits are a soft mold-formed plastic bait that comes in various sizes and shapes. They can be bought pre-rigged with hooks built into them but most anglers in the Northwest tend to use a 3 to

5-inch swimbait that requires threading onto a 4/0 to 7/0 hook with a lead shad-style jig head. The molds for the lead heads and plastic swimbaits are easy to get and many people have learned to pour their own. But if you're like me and have too many things to do, using commercially produced lead heads and swimbaits are the way to go.

I have fished numerous brands of fish trap lures and have found the Big Hammer swimbaits to be a great choice. Most swimbaits will be torn and unusable after the first fish, but Big Hammer's swimbaits tend to be a little more durable and in many cases, will survive being chewed on by numerous tuna. Although if you get into a hot bite, tuna will tear up any swimbait rather quickly. Not a bad problem to have, so you should plan to have a minimum supply of 20 to 30 swimbaits in each of your favorite colors for a day offshore.

SWIMBAIT RIGGING

IF YOU'RE TROLLING SWIMBAITS, THEY SHOULD BE THREADED ONTO the hook where the hook comes out the back, centered in the middle of the top of the swimbait. If the hook is slightly off to one side, they won't troll properly and you'll be wasting your time. An easy way to determine how far to thread the swimbait before bringing the hook out is illustrated in the first picture above. Position the lead jig head at the flat end of the swimbait with the hook laying along the side. Make a note of where the bend in the hook is on the swimbait and use the end of the hook to mark a spot on the back of the swimbait. This is where the hook should come out. If you do it correctly, the swimbait will be snug against the jig head. If you come out too short, it will allow the swimbait to slide back. Some anglers like to use a little glue on the front of the swimbait and a little on the lead jig head to prevent this.

You have numerous choices for size of lead jig heads. When I was new at it, I had sizes ranging from 0.75 ounce up to 2.5 ounces. Today I have just two sizes—1ounce and 2 ounces. Keep it simple. These two sizes will work very effectively 95% of the time.

I haven't noticed, nor have I heard anyone mention, much of a difference in catch rates between painted and unpainted lead jig heads. I have however, seen a difference if the lead jig heads don't have eyes on them. Many of the boat fish tuna and other predators key in on the jig heads with large eyes. If you get in a hot bite and later realize that one of the eyes has fallen off, keep fishing it until it doesn't work anymore or the bite dies. Cabelas and Bass Pro both sell eyes that stick on to replace lost ones.

I prefer using jig heads with fine wire hooks. Most jig head manufacturers use Mustad fine wire hooks but occasionally you'll run across 2 to 2.5 ounce jig heads with a thicker, heavier hook. These hooks will sometimes rip swimbaits while threading them and they tend to tear out quicker.

If you're using swimbaits to run and gun for jumpers, it's not so critical if it's off to one side slightly. Just remember to use a minimum of 4–6 feet of 30 to 50-pound fluorocarbon leaders and whatever you do—don't use a swivel connecting the leader to the swimbait head! It might seem to work okay, but tying the leader directly will pay bigger dividends over the course of the day. I use my live bait rods with fluorocarbon topshots to troll swimbaits but

your regular troll rods will work as long as you back off the drags.

The rod and reel are not as critical when trolling swimbaits. Just about any rod will work and since they don't peel off much line or peel at a blistering pace, you can get away with using a reel that has a line guide. You still need plenty of drag but keep in mind that this is a 20 to 35-pound fish. You just don't reel them in and land them very fast.

I started out trolling these swimbaits slow running 1.5 to 4 miles per hour but I've since learned that your speed isn't that critical and you can still be successful however fast you prefer to go. I'll sometimes put a swimbait out in my normal clone spread and usually it's down the center and about 50 to 75 feet back. If you're just trolling only swimbaits, put them farther back than you'd normally do with clones. I put them 75 to 150 feet behind the boat and I rarely ever fish anything beyond 75 feet with my other lures. When trolling at slower speeds, tuna typically don't peel off much before you stop. If you're using swimbaits to find fish with the intention of converting the hookup to a wide-open bite using live bait or iron, I'd fish it closer to the boat such as 50 to 75 feet back. If your gear is way back behind the boat, it makes it tougher to convert the stop to a wide-open bite.

When trolling swimbaits and you hook up, you have your choice of continuing to troll 7-10 seconds, similar to trolling clones, or you can stop and try to convert to a wide-open bite. Whichever you choose to do, once you stop, let the other swimbaits just sink and only clear the rods that might be in the way or might get tangled. The rocking of the boat will cause the swimbaits to keep fishing and hopefully entice a strike. I've seen fish pick up the swimbait with such force that they bend the pole, while at other times when they pick it up, it looks like a light trout bite, just nibbling as they swim around with the swimbait in their mouth and then they realize they're hooked. I've given them a good hookset in that instance.

When I first started using these swimbaits, I had a dozen colors in two to three sizes of each color consuming a couple of good-sized tackle drawers. After a few years of fishing these, I've narrowed it down to three to four colors and two sizes of each, ranging from 3 to 5 inches.

You really just need one or two dark colored and a couple light colored swimbaits. On most days, I can catch them with either a Walleye Whacker or Channel Island Chovey color.

Big Hammer – Deep Purple # 39

Big Hammer – Walleye Whacker #2

Big Hammer – Green Sardine #34

Fish Trap Lures – Channel Island Chovey

Running and Gunning with Swimbaits

If you like sight fishing, you'll like running and gunning for jumpers. It can be challenging, but it's a lot of fun. I've used it to hook fish and get a wide open bite going on numerous occasions.

A few years back, I had a writer onboard wanting to do an article on late season tactics—running and gunning for jumpers as well as working the iron. I had two other guys along who also had never done this, so it would be a new experience for them as well.

One of the guys asked if he could bring anything so I told him to pick up two packages of frozen calamari from the grocery store. I was going to use it for chum.

We ran southwest out of Garibaldi to the area known as Tuna Town located at 45N X 125W. It's known to hold tuna most of the summer and I'd had reports of good numbers of fish, so that was our intended destination.

I put one pack of frozen calamari in a bucket of seawater to thaw during the ride out. The other pack went in the cooler to stay frozen, hoping we wouldn't need it.

The ocean was like a lake that day which helps to spot jumpers. White capping wind waves would've made it difficult to spot them and can also make it difficult to stay on fish. We had a nice ocean and after a 50-mile run to the southwest, we soon spotted tuna jumping.

There are two rod holders mounted against my forward fish boxes making it a very convenient place to have a couple rods readily available for someone to walk up to the front of the boat and cast unobstructed. Having a center console boat is a benefit as it's easier to take part in run and gun casting from the front of the boat.

You have a lot of choices when it comes to casting rods and reels, whether you use a conventional bait casting reel or a spin reel. Spin reels have changed a lot over the past few years and are gaining in popularity again.

I prefer to use eight-foot, 15 to 30-pound class spin rods paired up with Daiwa 4500 (or larger) Saltiga spin reels, spooled with 30-pound braid, and topped off with a short section of 30-pound fluorocarbon leader tied directly to the lead jig head.

The writer had his camera in hand so I sent one of my friends to the front to cast a swimbait out to the jumper. I instructed him to cast as soon as he thought he could reach the tuna. I slowed the boat and took it out of gear as we slid closer to where we'd seen it jumping. It helps to get out in front of jumpers and try to intercept them, but at the least, you want to slide up to them quietly.

After a few failed attempts to hook a jumper, we went looking for another fish and didn't have to go far as there were jumpers in most any direction we looked. This was September and generally you'll find them jumping when you get in an area holding fish.

I had my friend go forward and get ready to cast while I positioned the boat. No one onboard had experienced this style of fishing and everyone had that dead serious look on his face. They were focused and intent on learning how to hook jumpers. But sometimes it doesn't have to be so serious. I had noticed that my buddy had brand new, shiny, bright yellow rubber bibs on, and I decided to have a little fun with him and told him that he had to get down on his knees because he was scaring the fish. I said he had to hide and get down to where he could just barely see over the gunnel, and he did. Once we were within casting distance, he let it fly and after letting the swimbait settle 10 to 20 seconds, started his retrieve. Nothing. "Do it again," I yelled, "and let it sink 20 to 30 seconds." Peeking over the gunnel, he let'er fly again, letting it sink longer before cranking the swimbait in. I finally walked forward and told him to stand up as the tuna could care less about his bright bibs. Think about it—he's a small dot compared to the 15,000 pound boat sliding through the water. My buddy and the rest of the group laughed and lightened up after that, and realized fishing didn't have to be so serious all the time.

I took his rod and cast it out again letting it sink 20 seconds before, ever so slowly, turning the handle on the spin reel and hooking the tuna on the second turn of the handle. I handed the rod back to my buddy and mentioned to him that he was reeling the swimbait back too fast. If you lay the swimbait on the water and barely move them, you'll notice they're swimming great. But this is where a lot of people make the mistake of reeling them in too fast. Slow down. Sometimes it pays to vary the speed, but in most cases, barely turning the handle and reeling slowly will work much better for you.

Remember, it's not a race—you're trying to catch a fish. That hookup led to a wide-open bite working the iron, which I'll cover in another chapter.

Many times while on a wide-open bite, I'll cast a swimbait out and put it in a rod holder. It's good to have another bait in the water and in most cases, there's a little drift, which keeps it out away from the boat enough distance to prevent tangles with hooked fish.

I almost always have some type of chum onboard to use to try to get the fish into a wide-open bite and this particular trip I didn't have live anchovies available and chose to use food grade calamari from the grocery store as my chum.

It just took two handfuls of ¼-inch size chopped up calamari to get the tuna into a feeding frenzy around the boat and after a two-hour stop, we were done.

Working the Iron

THE TITLE OF THIS TOPIC MIGHT LEAD YOU BELIEVE WE ARE chucking iron at fish but like many things, it's just a catch phrase for a technique that's been used for many years in Southern California, as well as other places where tuna have been fished for decades. The folks who partake in this style of fishing are commonly referred to as "iron workers." Wikipedia's definition of an iron worker is: A tradesman (man or woman) who works in the ironworking industry. *Sport Fishing Magazine's* definition is: Experts at choosing and using long slabs of shiny metal to hook a nearly limitless variety of game fish at all depths.

Since anglers in the Northwest are relatively new to the fishery that's been here for many years, we are a little late to the game. But as they say, "Better late than never," and boy, are we making up for lost time!

Shimano brought a lot of attention to fishing iron when they introduced their Butterfly Jig System a few years ago. It was expensive and didn't gain a lot of traction for a while until a few anglers bought into the system. I was one of those who had to give it a whirl since that dreaded memory of coming home empty-handed years earlier was lingering in the back of my mind, reminding me to always be open to a new technique.

On my last trip to the Fred Hall Show in Long Beach, I took a few minutes to visit my friend Steve Carson, in Southern California. Steve's a legend in tuna circles and he's been slinging iron since the late 60s. I'd say that's enough time to learn what works and what doesn't and to refine his technique to an art. Although our visit was short, I was reminded again why working the iron can be so successful and why Steve is one of the best at it.

One of the things I've noticed among anglers in the Northwest is we have those who really like to cast surface iron and we have those who prefer to work it vertically. You don't see too many folks who do both equally. I would fall in the latter category as I generally work it vertically more than casting it.

I can tell you from experience that there is not a faster method of catching tuna and loading the boat than vertically working iron—other than using a jack pole. You hook them, bring them over the side, and once you get unhooked, your jig goes right back over the side again. If you have them in a feeding frenzy, the jig will only be back in the water but a few seconds before you'll be hooked up again. It doesn't even have to do much but just fall back in the water, flutter once or twice, and you'll be tugging on Charlie.

CASTING

SURFACE IRON

IF YOU CHOOSE TO TRY CASTING SURFACE IRON, YOU'LL WANT A nice long rod paired up with a reel that has a floating spool, if you go with a conventional style reel. Conventional reels with star drags tend to be almost totally free-spool making them a good choice over lever drag reels when choosing a reel. Spin reels have

changed a lot over the past few years and are worthy of a look if that's what you prefer to use. Whichever way you go, you'll want something that will hold 250–300 yards of line.

Saltist H-C Levelwind Casting STTLW20H-C

I use 50-pound TUF-Line braid with a long topshot. A long topshot of 100 yards of fluorocarbon versus something shorter that has splices or joints is sometimes used to help keep things from hanging up on guides when line is coming off the spool at a high rate of speed. I've seen a few jigs go sailing, never to come back, after hearing the loud pop when a connection caught in the line guide. I've also used 4–6 feet of fluorocarbon topshot tied directly to the braid and when doing this, you just need to be careful to leave the connection outside the guides before casting. I use a Double Albright aka Improved Albright knot (page 84) and it makes a very small, smooth connection but at times will still catch in a guide.

Using iron to run and gun for jumpers is as effective, if not more at times, as swimbaits. Cast the jig out and let it flutter, free falling. If it stops falling or you feel the fish pick it up, set the hook. Sometimes it'll feel like a light trout bite and other times it will just stop falling. Half the time they'll pick it up on the drop. If it fails to get bitten on the drop, let it drop to well below a 45 degree angle, reel it back as fast as you can, and hold on. Sometimes you'll be cranking away and it will come up tight.

If you're not getting bitten or you want to mix it up a little, try stopping the jig while on the drop for a brief second every five seconds or so by using your thumb on the spool. You can also mix it up on the retrieve by pausing momentarily every few cranks.

There are a lot of jigs to pick from when shopping for surface iron but a few of the more common producers are Tady, Megabait, Shimano Flat-Side, and Diamond jigs. Jigs usually weigh 45–100 grams and are 1.5–4 inches in length. I prefer pink or pink combinations but blue or green combinations will also work.

Megabait

Tady

Some lures come pre-rigged with treble hooks of which I am not a big fan, primarily due to the extra barbs and the risk of hooking more than just the fish. They can be hazardous and difficult to remove from thumbs or other parts while bobbing around 50 miles offshore. They do have advantages though, when trying to entice a strike. A treble hook can cause a lure to flutter more due to the extra drag of the hooks going through the water. I tend to prefer a 4/0 siwash hook attached with a split ring. I generally don't rig surface iron with assist hooks on top such as when vertical jigging unless I'm casting a Shimano Flat Sided jig or possibly another jig that I would normally use for vertical jigging.

VERTICAL JIGGING

LATE IN THE SEASON, WHEN THE TUNA ARE COMMONLY FOUND ON the sonar in thermoclines 35–70 feet down, vertical jigging iron is often the only way to get down to them. Many times when we'd see jumpers, I'd have someone get up front and pitch a swimbait or iron to the tuna and if they successfully hooked up, we'd try to convert that to a wide-open bite. The last couple of years, I've changed tactics and don't even troll or try to cast to jumpers. If I see a jumper, I just stop on it and immediately drop iron. If the tuna are there, they'll usually show up on the sonar which will also give you the depth to drop your iron down into the range where they are. Vertical jigging is one of the best ways to bring the school up to the surface.

On a late season trip in October 2014, I was running offshore and was almost to my intended starting location for the day when we spotted a jumper, and by the time I got the throttles pulled back, we were on top of where we'd last seen it jump. I looked on the sonar and the tuna were down about 45 feet, prompting us to drop iron while throwing chum. We hooked up immediately, turning that stop into a three-hour marathon of yarding tuna over the side.

If you decide to give it a try, it's a lot of fun. In the beginning, vertical jigging will seem like a lot of work, but once you get the routine down, it becomes easier. Learning the technique and becoming successful with it will give you a tremendous sense of accomplishment. A lot of people pass on trying it because they think it's a lot of work and in the beginning it may seem that way, but once you get the technique dialed in, it's not near as much work or effort. Like anything new, the learning curve is steep but it just takes some practice and you'll start hooking fish.

Vertical jigging is very specific and requires a parabolic rod paired up with a high-speed reel. Daiwa and Shimano both have entry-level jig rods below $100 that will work fine. Rods typically are rated by the size of the jigs you will be using and by the line class. I use Daiwa SAG-J60MHF Saltiga G Conventional Jigging Boat Rods with a line class rating of 20–55 pounds and a jig size range of 4¼–5½ ounces (80–160 grams). I have used a little lighter-rated rods for beginners as they are a little more forgiving when working the jig.

These rods are incredibly tough and the first time you're hooked up on a tuna, the rod will likely be doubled over but don't worry, it takes a lot to break one. One of the benefits of these parabolic rods is they shut off close to the reel which puts less stress on your back and at the end of the day when you've battled quite a few tuna, you'll be thankful you had it. The rods are powerful and have great hook-setting ability.

The next key component of this system is the reel and here's where you're going to spend some money. To get what you need, it will set you back a minimum of $250. If you try to cut corners and go cheap, you'll be disappointed out on the tuna grounds. A cheap reel may not retrieve line as fast as it needs to, or the drag system may not hold up, causing you to walk back into the tackle store and plunk down even more money to do it all over again,

Saltiga Hyper-Speed Lever Drag SALD35H

so... Don't go cheap! Buy good quality and get what you need the first time.

What are you looking for? You need a reel that has a high speed retrieve of 6:1 or faster and retrieves a minimum of 40 inches of line per turn of the handle; 45–48 inches is ideal. This is very critical and can mean the difference between catching fish or not. Daiwa designed their Saltiga Hyper Speed Lever Drag reel for jigging, which has a 7:1 ratio and retrieves a whopping 52 inches per crank, while also giving you the ability to slam the brakes on a long run with its 40 pounds of max drag. Today there are a lot of good reel manufacturers out there but when putting as much stress on the reel as you will when vertical jigging, go with a metal versus graphite. You don't need a two-speed reel for albacore but the difference between many of the reels is sometimes only a few ounces and a few dollars. And you can also use this reel when traveling and fishing for other species of fish that might require the ability to drop down a gear.

Spool the reel with 250–300 yards of line, then add a fluorocarbon topshot and you're ready to go. I use the Saltiga 35 size and spool it with 280 yards of 65- pound TUF-Line, leaving just enough room to attach 20 feet of 50-pound Seaguar fluorocarbon. Why so heavy? When vertical jigging, the strike is more reactionary and this gives you the opportunity to scale up a little on your line and get the fish in the boat quicker.

I like to use the Double Albright knot for this connection due to its low profile and nice smooth flow through the guides. The only time I've ever had an issue with this connection is when I didn't get the knot tightened down enough, so make sure you get it nice and snug. It's not hard to tie, even on a rocking ocean when you need to replace a topshot. Wind-on topshot leaders are also an easy way to change out a broken leader.

Some guys like to use a longer topshot

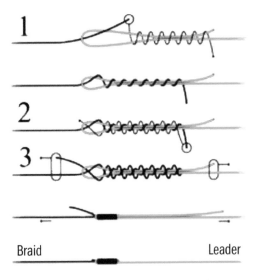

Braid   Leader

Improved or Double Albright

to help sort out tangles when fish cross lines, and there have been a few times when I wished I had used a longer one, too. On one occasion, we were offshore late in the fall and had only a few fish in the box when the bite kicked in around 2 p.m. We soon had a wide-open bite going and we weren't into the bite for very long when our lone, inexperienced fisherman failed to follow his fish, and before we could do anything, I was staring over the side at a knotted mess. I put my reading glasses on just so I could see a clearer picture of what I had to deal with, and after 20 minutes of trying to untangle braid and fluorocarbon, I realized it was useless. I put on heavy leather gloves and hand-lined each fish up to the boat. Another person gaffed the fish and I cut the line. We did this with all four fish. In many cases you'd lose your bite, but we quickly grabbed the extra rods and dropped new baits overboard back into hungry fish, taking up where we left off.

After a great day on the water with lots of action, make sure you check the topshot for nicks and frays. You might even want to check it while you're fishing if the action is hot and heavy. I've cut off 4–6 inches right above the jig and re-tied the jig on many occasions during the day.

You have many choices for jigs and most of them will catch tuna. If your local tackle shop doesn't carry them, you only have to surf the internet to find all types and sizes out there. Shimano Flat Sided jigs are the most common and work very well, although they are expensive. It's not uncommon to lose one from time to time, so it pays to have a few extras pre-rigged and ready in the event you lose one while on a wide-open bite. I get asked many times, "What size jigs should I buy?" Jigs used for vertical jigging in the waters off the Northwest will generally range from 90–180 grams. I fish a lot of jigs in the 110–140 gram sizes but on those windy days or days with a lot of current drift, you might need to change out to a larger jig to get it to go down without having a lot of scope in the line. This logic would then lead you back to needing more than one size when buying jigs.

Flutter Jigs vs. Standard Jigs - Standard jigs typically have to drop and then be worked, causing it to attract strikes. Flutter jigs work both directions, attracting strikes on the drop as well as when being retrieved. When Shimano introduced the Butterfly jig system, the jig was standard iron, but within a few years, many of the jig manufacturers started kicking out jigs that could work both directions, Flutter jigs. When using Flutter jigs that work both directions, many days you'll catch as many fish on the drop as you do working the jig on the retrieve.

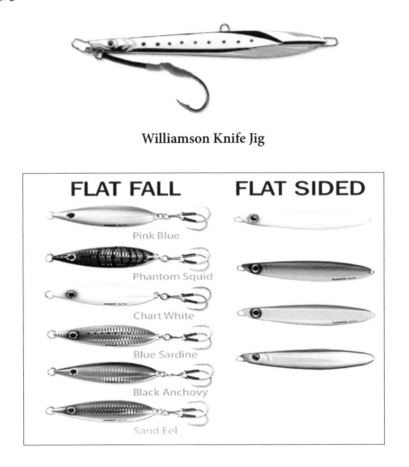

Williamson Knife Jig

Some years the sharks can be thick and it doesn't take long before they show up on a stop. Sharks also tend to be curious, so don't leave your jig just dangling in the water while you're distracted with your thumb in your ear, or they'll come along and pick it up. If they do, don't try to finesse them to the boat, but literally horse them up to the boat to get the jig. Screw around with them for too long and they'll start rolling, which will also ruin the fluorocarbon topshot. Most sharks are 3–4 feet long and small enough to deal with, but let a big 6-footer get a hold of the jig and good luck.

Rigging Vertical Iron - The first thing you attach to your lure to rig your vertical iron is a test-rated split ring. I prefer the Owner split rings in the 5.5–6.0 size for most lures that are 4–6 inches in length. To that attach a solid Owner ring in the 5.5–6.0 size and then tie it directly to your fluorocarbon topshot. Do not use a swivel—it's not needed. Now attach a size 2/0 rigged assist hook on one side, or if you prefer, you can add one to both sides, but attach it to the solid ring. I prefer using the Gamakatsu model 510 assist hooks, either pre-rigged or unrigged. Sometimes I'll make up my own assist hooks using a 2/0 Gamakatsu 510 and 9 inches of 200-pound test-rated Kevlar parachute cord. The size of the assist hooks is not a critical component of the equation if you've waited to the last minute to buy them and now it's tuna season and you can't locate a 2/0. No worries, just about any size from 1/0–5/0 will get it done.

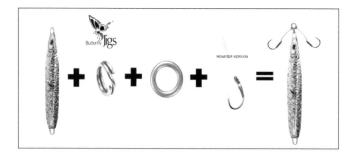

Once you have the rod and reel set up, it's time to put them to use. You can use a couple of different techniques to work the iron properly.

Speed Jigging - This technique involves having the rod handle up under your armpit with the reel cupped in one hand and then pumping the rod up and down while reeling. Every turn of the handle on the reel should correspond to one lifting or dropping motion of the rod. Some days tuna like a fast action and at other times it may seem like you're barely moving it when they take it and the rod comes up tight. When that happens, reel while lowering your rod tip and give it another snug lift while continuing to reel, making sure the tuna is hooked well. When you have fish located at a specific depth on the sonar, there's not much need to bring the jig all the way back to the surface each time. Work it up until you believe you're out of the range of depth where they're located, then drop it back down, stopping momentarily every five seconds.

Speed Reeling - Just as it implies, you're dropping the jig and then cranking it back as fast as you can. Just make sure you have a good grip on the rod because that lure is coming back fast and you need to be prepared for quite a jolt if it comes to an abrupt stop before getting all the way back to the boat.

Variety of Speed and Lift - Sharp, fast, erratic movement is the key to getting strikes. Sometimes that comes from using a combination of speed reeling mixed in with the pumping yo-yo action of the rod.

Dead Sticking - Drop the jig into the zone where the fish are showing up on the sonar, and put the rod in the gunnel rod holder, then let the boat work it as the swells create a rocking motion. Good luck getting it out of the rod holder!

THE NICE THING ABOUT WORKING THE IRON IS YOU CAN TARGET the fish once you've located them on the sonar. It's also one of the best methods to bring the whole school up to the surface as many times the school will follow a hooked fish upward.

Live Bait Fishing

Like many others, I learned to fish albacore by trolling in Mexico and Central America and while there, I caught many species of fish, including tuna, using live bait. But it wasn't till I joined a buddy on his boat that I really experienced the rush of watching a tuna taking a bait just a few yards in front of me.

That particular trip was June 17th out of Newport, Oregon. It was very early in the season by Oregon and Washington tuna fishing standards, but we had a window of good weather. We'd been wanting to fish together for a few years and as luck would have it, we both just happened to be in Newport at the same time, so we took the opportunity. My buddy had about 75 herring in his bait tank that he'd caught the day before, using Sabiki rigs. He had been fishing near the green buoy, slightly upstream of the Coast Guard station in Newport—a popular place to catch herring.

We had looked at sea surface temperatures the night before and had a good idea of where we thought we should start. The sun was just peeking up over the coast range as we slipped out of the harbor and made our way offshore, heading due west. We soon arrived at our intended target location and started out trolling six rods and right out of the gate, hooked up. It had been a long winter and we were rusty, way out of sync, and in the beginning weren't even trying to convert the stop to a live bait bite. After a while, we realized we weren't even prepared to convert to a bait stop since we had failed to rig any rods for live bait, and after scouring the boat for five minutes, failed to find any live bait hooks. Seems my buddy had cleaned out his onboard tackle trays at the end of the previous season and inadvertently forgot to put a few things back. This trip was an impromptu, last minute decision and neither one of us had been offshore for tuna that season, so it was also a shake down run. As luck would have it, I happened to be scheduled to give a tuna seminar the next day and had my seminar gear with me, which had one sample pack of three live bait hooks.

With 42 fish for the three of us, this trip ended by 1 p.m. only because we ran out of ice and storage space. You'd never guess by the number of fish that we caught that it was somewhat of a Chinese circus not having all the correct gear or being properly prepared. The live bait hooks I had were not even the right size for the big eight-inch baits we had, but they still worked. I have to come to believe that tuna are truly the ultimate predator and if it swims, they'll eat it. We'd hook a herring, toss it overboard, and wait only a few moments before a silver streak zipped by, inhaled the bait, and headed for waters unknown. After five seconds, the bail on the reel would get flipped into gear and the rod would almost leave your hands. Soon we had them darting and boiling everywhere behind the boat. A bait would hit the water and within seconds it would get inhaled. The feeding frenzy was incredible. It's this type of action that will really get you excited and makes many a tuna angler go crazy and become addicted. Welcome to the Dark Side.

That was quite a few years back and a great memory. Fishing for tuna, especially with live bait, is exciting, fast paced, and in the blink of an eye you can get multiple hookups with tuna going in every direction, and then just like that the bite can die. One moment you're on an exciting high and the next moment you're wondering what just happened. It's still as exciting today as my first experience, and the only difference is that I'm a little better equipped now for this style of fishing.

My first tuna trip offshore was in a boat not really designed or built for what I was doing with it. Over the years I've bought and sold a few other boats that were okay but not really the fishing machine like I have today. Aside from the obvious triple 300

Verados outboard engines and being long and sleek, the Hydra Sport is by far the best-built and equipped boat I have ever owned for running or fishing offshore.

Bait Tanks - A bait tank is a vital piece of equipment you'll need if you're going to fish live bait and spending a little time doing your research will save you some headaches. Not all bait tanks are created equal and there are many types and manufacturers of them. I have a 50-gallon bait tank made by Kodiak built into my bait prep station. HydraSports Custom offers your choice of their custom pressurized system or a Kodiak bait tank, which is also pressurized. Pressurized bait tanks have additional benefits including keeping the bait from getting banged up when running offshore in sporty seas. I've had six big scoops of anchovies in mine and after eight hours they were still very lively with very few dead floaters. Manufacturers in Southern California and out on the East Coast generally know what they're talking about and know how to set them up properly.

The tank should be round or preferably oval and have no corners or places for bait to congregate where they'll die from crowding from lack of oxygen. It should have a light inside making it easier for the bait to see where they're swimming. A light is also better for them if you're trying to keep them overnight to use the next day.

Water flow is one of the big factors as to whether your bait is going to be healthy or even survive the run to the tuna grounds. The tank should fill in eight minutes for best results. If it fills in nine minutes or longer, they may not get enough oxygen and die. Likewise, if it fills in seven minutes or faster, the flow could be so strong and fast they'll swim so hard, they die. I can regulate my flow in two places. One is by a valve before the pump, which I prefer not to do, as starving the pump by working it too much can possibly cause it to burn out. I prefer to regulate the flow by adjusting the outflow. Some guys will have a backup pump or system in the event they have an issue.

Water flows into my tank in a clockwise rotation and the bait will be schooled up in a circle headed into the flow. It's very important that you have a nice circular flow versus water randomly flowing straight into the tank.

Sea Chests - In the last few years, sea chests have become very popular and can alleviate flow issues as well as air locks. The water intake on the bottom of most boats generally has a clam shell fitting that catches water as the boat moves forward. They work fine until you back up, such as coming out of your slip or away from the bait station. Water moving past the clam shell in the opposite direction can cause the intake to catch air and lose its prime causing an air lock that sometimes is hard to get back without moving forward at a pretty good speed, possibly faster than allowed in the harbor. In spite of how good my Kodiak bait system is, I get an air lock almost every time I back out of my slip. I have learned to fill the bait tank prior to backing out and at the moment I'm ready to go, I turn off the pump while backing up. Once I stop and start moving forward, I turn the pump back on. Things seem to work fine with this process. Generally the tank only loses about 20% of the water and is still plenty full.

A sea chest inline is a good way to correct this air lock issue. A sea chest can be made in various sizes but it is basically a small rectangular box made out of fiberglass or aluminum with a clear plastic top allowing you to see inside where there are one or more submersible bilge pumps. The box is installed below the water line of the boat allowing it to fill naturally.

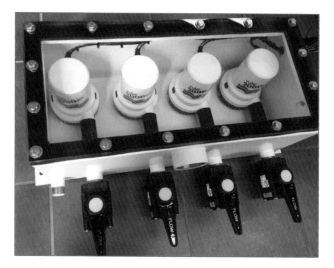

Sea Chest

Bait - Anchovies are the most common bait in the Northwest and one of the hardest baits to keep alive. They stress very easily so it's important to have a live well or bait tank system that works efficiently. Buying scoops of bait at a bait station is the easiest way to fill the bait tank but unfortunately there are only a few places in the Northwest where you can find them. Westport and Ilwaco are the only two places in Washington where you can get live anchovies and are also the most common ports where people run out of when live bait fishing for tuna. Winchester Bay has had bait in the past and Garibaldi is trying to make it available on a regular basis.

Take a look at the first scoop of bait to see how big they are and if they have red noses. If the baits are big you may not be able to hold as many. If they are average size but have red noses they may not be very healthy and you might need an extra scoop to make up for the ones that die off. Periodically remove the dead floaters and toss them in a bucket to use for chum if needed.

If you fish out of a port that doesn't have a bait station you can always try to catch your own bait using a throw net. A lot of times you can find schools of bait in the bay or just outside the harbor. If you try a throw net, take the time to practice throwing it on land, such as in your driveway or yard.

If a throw net is not your style, you can use a Sabiki rig on a rod. Once you locate a school of anchovies and start hooking them, make sure you touch the baits as little as possible. The best method of removing them from the hook is to hold the bait over the tank, then take the hook and turn it out of the bait, allowing it to drop into the tank without touching it. If finding bait is difficult, try using lights at night to attract them. I've heard of some folks who broadcast a small amount of dry cat food to attract them. Keep in mind that if you're catching herring as well as anchovies, don't throw them back. Remember, if it swims, a tuna will eat it.

Be careful running offshore on a sporty ocean with a full bait tank. It doesn't make much sense to go to all the effort of catching bait or spending good money on them only to kill them off running hard on a rough ocean. Slow down a little and give them a smoother ride—you'll appreciate it as well.

Gear - I've seen people use quite a variety of rods for live bait and there's nothing set in stone as to what you have to use to be successful. I prefer a seven-foot rod for a couple of reasons. Most anglers are novices at fly-lining a bait away from the boat and a short rod has a tendency to let the bait go back under the boat because it falls into the water so close to the boat. A longer rod is too hard to handle a tuna when you have multiple anglers hooked up and you're trying to move around. It's also a pain to untangle lines with longer rods. I have used a number of rods over the years for live bait but in the last few years, one of my crew members on my tournament team has been using a seven-foot Lamiglas Tri-Flex rod designed and sold to guys fishing stripers on the East Coast. These rods are lightweight and tough. My crew member fishes a lot of people on his boat who have never fished tuna and who have wrapped the rods around the edge of the boat and have flat abused them at times. In the five to six years that he's used these rods, he's only broken the tip off one and the guide off another; a real testament of how tough these rods are.

Lamiglas has since made my crew and me our own rods with our logos and per my request, changed the looks of the rod to a blue finish with rubber grips versus the cork that was on the previous models. I have since had them make me troll rods and a spin rod in the same look and design. I have recently been working with them on a new "Tuna Dog" series of bluewater series rods, designed on those blanks.

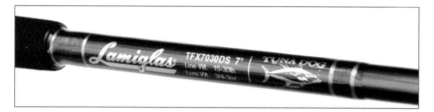

Lamiglas TFX7030DS Tuna Dog Series Live Bait Rod

The reel you put on your rod should be of good quality and have a very smooth drag. Most anglers prefer an open face lever drag reel. I use Daiwa Saltiga SALD20-2SPD Lever drag reels. You don't need two-speed reels but if you travel to other places it might come in handy fishing other species. A good quality reel is going to cost you some money—upwards of $250—but if you don't make the investment you'll be back buying another reel after a few trips. If you're fishing on a budget, a lever drag reel that you would use for jigging iron will also work for live bait fishing. The braided line will also work for either scenario although you might have to change the fluorocarbon topshot to a lighter weight such as 30-pound test when being used for live bait fishing.

Albacore are hard on drags and reel components when they make short bursts peeling line off at a blistering pace. My first experience was with a star drag reel and when I flipped the bail engaging the drag, the rod almost came out of my hands. It was quite a jolt on the drag system and line. If I'd had a weak link somewhere it would've come apart. I would stay away from a star drag reel or a reel with a line guide which will also have a star drag.

Daiwa Saltiga SALD20-2SPD

When reeling an open face reel, pay attention to how the line is coming back on the reel and move it back and forth on the spool with your fingers helping it to wind on evenly, or the spool might build up on one end to the point it won't reel anymore.

You have a couple of choices of how you spool the reel depending on what size reel you choose. I like a small size 20 reel and because of that, I will spool it with 200 yards of 50-pound TUF-Line High Vis braided line. As long as you have 200–300 yards of line on the reel you'll be fine. If you're using braided line with a topshot, the size of the braid isn't as critical, but I wouldn't drop below 50-pound test. Some anglers fish heavier braid because it gives them more abrasion resistance and it handles better when it gets tangled. It's not a matter of *if* you'll ever get tangled, it's *when*. If you fish braided line, it's a good idea to have a thick pair of leather gloves onboard to

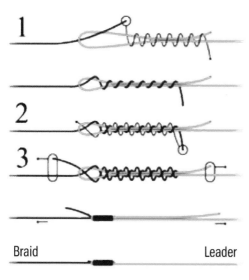

Braid　　　　　　　　　　　　Leader

Improved or Double Albright

hand-line fish to the boat if needed.

Your other option is to buy a big spool of fluorocarbon and spool the reel with 200–300 yards of 30-pound fluorocarbon. You might have to shop around but several manufacturers make spools of it. It makes it easier to sort out tangles.

I prefer smaller reels and therefore use braided line to get enough on the spool which means I have to add a fluorocarbon topshot. I use a Double Albright knot to attach 20 feet of Seaguar fluorocarbon leader. This is one of the best knots for tying two lines together of different diameters. Some anglers like to use a Double Uni-Knot but it tends to have bigger knots and doesn't go through the guides as well.

Most years I use 30-pound fluorocarbon but in 2015 the fish were not line shy and I used 50-pound topshots. Some years they will

be line shy and you might have to drop down in leader size. But it's been quite a few years since we've had to drop down to 20 pounds.

I have used many different fluorocarbon leaders and in the last couple of years started using Seaguar fluorocarbon. Fluorocarbon tends to be stiff, but Seaguar is by far one of the softest and easiest to tie, making it especially nice when trying to tie on those small hooks.

Gamakatsu Ringed Live Bait Hook

Also, make sure you check your leader for frays after every fish and cut off a little if needed, then tie the hook back on.

Live bait hooks should be sized to match the size of the bait you're using. Anchovies are the most common bait available in the Northwest. Since they tend to be 3–4 inches and occasionally up to 5–6 inches long such as in 2015, a #1 or #2 hook size, depending on the manufacturer, would be appropriate. I prefer Gamakatsu ringed live bait hooks, which allow the bait to swim freely and look more natural. Make sure you have a good supply of hooks—when the action is fast and furious you'll burn through quite a few. On a day when boating 30–50 fish, we'll go through 10–25 hooks, and there have been a few days when sharks were a problem where we used twice that.

You might want to have some extra live bait rods ready. My job as the skipper is also to be the deck hand and I always have a rigged rod ready for someone who breaks off a fish, or just lands one but the leader is frayed, so it's going to take a few minutes to cut off the bad section and tie on a new hook.

If you can't find ringed live bait hooks, you can still tie them on with a Perfection Loop Knot. This is the most common knot used to tie hooks as it leaves a loop allowing the bait to swim without any hindrance.

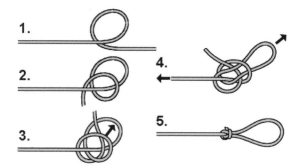

Perfection Loop for Non-Ringed Live Bait Hooks

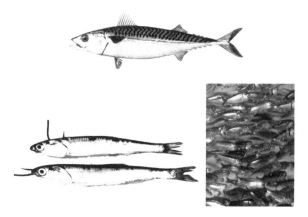

Albacore Tuna

Now that you have everything rigged, it's time to fish. Using a small bait net, try to get the liveliest bait in the tank. There are a number of ways to hook a bait and they all have their advantages and disadvantages. I hook them through the nose sideways or in the back near the dorsal fin area. Hooking through the lower jaw and going up through their nose works well and prevents their mouth from coming open if you need to reel the bait back to the boat. If the tuna are down deeper, you can hook the bait near the anal fin causing them to swim downward. If they don't swim down, I place a ¼–½ ounce inline sinker about 3 feet up the line. You want the bait to go down gently— it's hard on them if it's too much weight and drags them down too fast.

Now it's time to go find some fish. I mentioned earlier in this book that I rarely troll now and instead, I use my electronics much more to find fish once I get in an area that's showing signs that there could be tuna. If you're not comfortable relying on your electronics, you might prefer the old fashioned method of trolling to find fish. If you're trolling or trying to locate fish and you come across another boat dead in the water, don't get very close to them or you could cause them to lose their bite. I'd give them a good 300-yard buffer. If they call you on the radio and invite you into their bite, that's different, but don't slide in uninvited or you might create enemies and be subject to their verbal wrath on the radio.

DEL STEPHENS

Converting a Troll-Caught Fish to Wide-Open Bite

I used to troll to find fish and the first thing you need to understand is that timing is critical if you're hoping to convert a troll-caught fish to a wide-open live bait bite.

Before we ever start trolling, I give everyone onboard a designated job. Since this is going to be a team effort, if everyone does their job as instructed, things should work out great. I use a couple of different techniques to get the bite wide open.

At the sound of the singing clicker signaling a hookup, I will bring the throttles into neutral and then into reverse, stopping our forward momentum. This prevents the tuna from running very far on the troll rod, keeping us closer to the school of tuna. My job as skipper is to clear the rods. I typically start out trolling with only three to four rods instead of a five or six rod spread. It takes less time to clear three to four rods once we hook up.

I will have one person designated to throw chum and once we hook a troll fish, that person's job is to quickly grab the bait net, scoop a handful of bait, then smack their hand against the back of the net sending the bait over the rail into the water. This stuns the anchovies momentarily, giving the tuna a chance to get on them before they dart back under the boat trying to hide. I will have the boat's forward momentum stopped by the time they get the chum overboard.

While I'm getting the boat stopped, the other anglers are supposed to be doing their jobs. One of them is casting a drop back rig in the direction of the troll hooked fish. That might be a swimbait or possibly a small iron on a spin rod. If they don't hook up, they flip the bail of the reel and put it in a rod holder and get a live bait rod baited and overboard as quickly as possible. Two others are getting iron rods, dropping iron jigs overboard, and working the iron while the other anglers are getting their live bait rods baited and overboard.

Why use iron? You don't have to bait iron so it makes sense to get it working right away to start hooking fish. This then helps to get the school of tuna going and consequently, get the live bait rods hooking up. All of this needs to happen very fast and preferably in the first 30 seconds of the troll hooked fish. Some anglers call it the "magic minute"—a good description of this brief and exciting time.

If you have a big boat with a flybridge that catches the wind such as on my other crew member's boat, it might be more difficult to work iron. In that case, we stop the boat ASAP and throw chum while one or two people are throwing a drop back rig. The others are baiting live bait rods and quickly getting the baits into the water.

Remember what I said earlier in the book about how everyone's boat fishes differently and how all anglers have their own style of how they like to fish? So it just may be that you don't want to fish iron when you're fishing live bait, and that's okay.

Once I've stopped the boat and cleared the lines, hopefully the others are hooking up. My boat will now be drifting sideways to the wind and swell where the anglers will all be on the rail with the wind in their face. Once in a while someone will drop a bait on the downwind (wrong) side and that generally leads to tangles unless I catch them before they get bitten. Stay on the upwind side of the boat with the wind in your face and spread out if you can. This is where my center console boat really works well since anglers can spread out along the rail giving themselves plenty of room.

The people on live bait rods will have the lever drag on the reel backed all the way off and the rod tip pointed in the direction of their bait. It's best to strip a couple of good arm lengths of line off the reel to help keep the bait from ending up right beside the boat. On days with a lot of wind drift, you might have quite a bit of line out. When a tuna comes streaking by, your bait will get very nervous and many times you can feel them swimming harder to avoid becoming a meal. Many times they don't get the chance to do anything but get wet before Charlie is on them and the bait has been inhaled. Once line is streaking off the reel, you'll want to count for about five seconds and then slowly ease the lever drag up about halfway to the strike position. The rod will load up and line will still be coming off at a good pace but DO NOT SET THE HOOK! Allowing the tuna to inhale the bait for five seconds, then easing the drag up, will generally cause the hook to anchor in their jaw when the line comes tight and is well hooked. If you try to set the hook, you run the risk of breaking the line and snapping the fish off.

Generally, the tuna will stop running after the first short burst and now you can run the drag all the way up to the strike position. If you get a tuna that swims directly under the boat near the running gear, just back the drag off completely where they can't feel drag and wait 30 seconds. They'll swim back out and when you run the drag back up, they'll be right out in front of you most of the time.

If I'm fishing people who are novices, I leave the clickers on to give the reel a slight tension or they might birds nest the spool when a tuna takes the bait. Once hooked up, they can switch the clicker off.

Hopefully by now you've got multiple fish hooked up but they're going in multiple directions. Follow your fish whatever you do. We call it "doing the dance," and if you don't, it'll lead to chaos and tangles. Go down the rail under others and over others, switching places if needed to keep your fish in front of you. Try to keep your fish on one side of the boat. A fish that gets on the other side of the boat will tangle with others on that side and mess everybody up. If multiple fish are hooked and one of them is out away from the boat, don't reel that one in right away. Instead, land some of the others that are closer in while keeping some distance between the fish. Just be sure to keep a little tension on that farther fish. It can seem like orchestrated chaos at times, but if you work together doing the dance, you'll land most of your fish without too many issues. That's part of the allure that makes live bait fishing so exciting.

If the bite is going wide open, you might not need to chum any further. I don't always continue chumming unless the bite slows. I have at times, thrown a couple of good scoops of bait out to get the tuna into a good feeding frenzy and then nothing until the bite slows down. If the bite slows and you need to throw more chum, typically you should only throw three to five anchovies and toss them over the rail on the downwind side of the boat so the boat drifts over the top of them. If the bite is just mediocre with a fish here and there being hooked, you'll want to continue chumming every few minutes tossing just a couple of anchovies at a time as before.

If you don't get the bite going after the troll hooked a fish, keep working it for 10–15 minutes, then go back on the troll.

I donate a few charity trips each year and on one of those trips, we asked our three guests how many tuna they'd like to keep. Never having experienced a feeding frenzy, they each remarked that six fish apiece seemed like a good day. I looked at my wife who helps on most of those trips and chuckled thinking, *Eighteen fish—this will be a piece of cake!*

We had been whacking them on a consistent basis and were headed back to one of our recent productive locations. We didn't get very far offshore when we came across a kelp patty and tossed a swimbait which immediately got bitten and got our hopes up that we'd get things going now. But after working the area over for 20 minutes with nothing else to show for our effort, we picked up and continued to our original intended location.

Once we arrived and started trolling looking for fish, we went over everyone's roles. It wasn't very long before we hooked up and everyone went into their routines. They did it perfectly but after 10 minutes, we only had the troll-caught fish. We continued back on the troll and time and time again, we'd hook a single or a double and everyone would go into their designated routine. At noon, I looked at my wife and shook my head in disbelief. We had 10 tuna in the box and what originally seemed like a short, easy day was looking more like a long day of just picking them off one or two at a time.

Then it happened—hooked up again. But this time it went wide open and for the next hour our guests never got a break. It was one fish after another and most of the time there were three fish hooked at any given moment. I was gaffing, then cutting them to bleed, but they were coming over the rail so fast I couldn't keep up and soon the 30-gallon garbage can bleed bucket was full with 10–12 tuna and there were another 10–12 on the floor around me. Our guests would get one in and go right back over for another one.

Finally I mentioned that they had way more fish than they originally intended and they could stop any time they wanted. They were all worn out but were not about to give up until I mentioned how many fish they had landed, and then with a huge sigh of relief, decided to stop.

Sometimes it takes a few attempts to get the bite going even though our guests were performing their roles perfectly each time. Just because you don't get it going the first few times, don't get yourself down—keep after it. Practice it, practice it, and keep practicing it and then boom—it'll go. We had six to seven attempts that day before it went wide open right after lunch.

Wide-open bites are what tuna anglers live for and just as quickly as you get them going, they can die. On another charity trip, we got them going on the first stop and after a while, I noticed the guys were getting worn out and decided they needed a sandwich. That's a good way to lose your bite, which is what happened on that trip, as after we had something to eat, we never got it going again, although we already had plenty of fish. But when you have the bite wide open, you need to make hay while you can because the bite can still die even if everyone is still working it. I've had wide-open bites that lasted for hours until we were too full to hold any more fish, and I've had the bite die after only a couple fish. There's never a guarantee of how long it will last.

Chumming

Chumming is a very effective way to get the bite going allowing you to fish in one place, dead in the water, using live bait fishing or working the iron.

Keep in mind you don't always have to chum just because you have it available. I've had trips offshore where we hooked a fish on the troll and converted it to a wide-open bite and never threw any chum. I've also hooked fish down deep and with four people working the iron, we had the fish going for hours without using any chum. I would encourage you to have chum onboard and available if you can, because there will be a time when you need it to get the fish going.

The two most common products used for chumming in the Northwest are live anchovies and "individually quick frozen" dead anchovies, or IQF, as they are known. The IQF are typically sold in 20 to 40-pound boxes and commonly used a lot by the commercial fleet.

There are plenty of other things that will also work for chum. I've seen people take herring or squid and chop them up into small ¼–½ inch pieces. On one trip, I created a feeding frenzy using a couple of handfuls of food grade calamari from the grocery store, chopped into ¼ inch pieces.

Commercial chum can also be used and is available from some of the seafood processors. The only thing I don't like about commercial chum is that the blood in it will sometimes attract sharks. The sharks will probably show up anyway, but the blood will draw them in sooner than you want, sometimes killing a good bite.

Friskies dry cat food has also been used, but the last thing I want on my boat is bits of dry cat food that can get scattered here and there only to get wet and make a mess. A bloody mess on the boat is one thing, but sticky cat food stuck to the textured floor is a real pain to deal with when the day is done and you're trying to clean the boat.

Once in a while you'll hear of someone using popcorn. The tuna don't come up to eat it, but the birds love it and the tuna will come up to see what the birds are working on. Just another way to trick the tuna, like spraying the ocean with your wash down hose to simulate bait jumping out of the water.

Think that's bizarre? I have a friend who cooked up a big bucket of elbow macaroni, dyed it pink to look like shrimp, and even added a little scent to make it authentic. He says it works. I've fished beside him and he *was* catching fish. He is one of the most ingenious guys I know and has tried numerous other things which I won't mention, just to help keep a few of his secrets, secret.

Chum can also work to bring fish up from down below. I've seen folks throw chum out while trolling in a circle, throwing the chum inside the circle as they troll around the outside.

I fish out of a port that has live anchovies and generally use that as my chum. I like to throw a couple of good-sized handfuls of live anchovies right away and once we get the bite going, I back off and throw a couple of individual anchovies every couple of minutes. The last thing you want to do is to keep throwing too much food, causing the bite to die off because you've filled them up with chum.

When broadcasting live bait, I like to use a bait net to scoop up 10–15 baits and then whack the back of the net with my hand, stunning the bait, and sending them overboard. Because the anchovies are temporarily stunned, the tuna have a chance to get on them before they recover and swim under the boat to hide.

I've had many days where we were working the iron and once we got the fish going with the first few handfuls of chum, we never used any after that. And there have been many other times when working the iron, where we not only didn't have to use chum to get the tuna going, but also didn't need any to keep them on the bite.

DEL STEPHENS

Taking Care of the Catch

Characteristics of Albacore and Other Tunas

Albacore, and all other tunas, have higher body temperatures than salmon, rockfish, and most other fishes. When landed, the body temperature of most other fishes is the same as the water temperature. But a recent study found that the backbone temperature of troll-caught albacore ranged from 75°F to 92°F and averaged 84.5°F. An average albacore was 25°F warmer than the temperature of the surface waters where they were caught. Actual body temperature depends on fish size, the extent to which the fish struggled during capture, and water temperature.

Decomposition or spoilage is caused primarily by the chemical breakdown of the flesh by enzymes produced by naturally occurring bacteria. This spoilage process is faster at higher temperatures and proceeds more rapidly in warm albacore than in cold-blooded fishes.

Albacore store energy in chemical compounds such as adenosine triphosphate (ATP). While the albacore is alive, ATP is used for swimming and other cellular needs. It is replenished through a process requiring oxygen. As albacore struggle during capture, they deplete their supply of ATP and oxygen and begin to produce ATP through an alternate pathway that also produces lactic acid. They also generate more heat than their temperature-control mechanism can handle.

After death, albacore can naturally no longer regulate body temperature or flesh pH (acidity/alkalinity). ATP is broken down by enzymes to compounds that are associated with off-flavors in "stale" fish, flesh temperature remains high, and the flesh remains slightly acidic. The harder an albacore struggles during capture and/or thrashing around on deck, the higher the flesh temperature and acidity. Poor handling after capture can easily result in rapid loss of quality and decomposition.

Scombroid Poisoning

Albacore and other tunas contain relatively large amounts of the amino acid histidine in their flesh (amino acids are the building blocks of proteins). After the fish dies, bacterial enzymes break down the histidine to histamine. Humans consuming fish containing histamine can become ill with scombroid poisoning. Symptoms include a metallic, sharp, or peppery taste in the mouth after eating the fish, nausea, vomiting, abdominal cramps and diarrhea, oral blistering and numbness, facial swelling and flushing, headache and dizziness, palpitations, hives, rapid and weak pulse, thirst, and difficulty in swallowing. Most victims of scombroid poisoning recover within 24 hours; antihistamines usually lead to immediate improvement. Fish most often implicated in this illness include: tuna, bluefish, mackerel, and bonito.

In 1993, there were several cases of scombroid poisoning reported in Newport, Oregon, from unfrozen albacore sold from a fishing vessel to a restaurant. In order for histamine to form in the fish, the albacore had to be mishandled at some point between capture and consumption. The best way to prevent scombroid poisoning is rapid chilling on the vessel and controlling the temperature of the fish throughout storage and distribution. Once histamine forms in a fish, it cannot be eliminated by cooking, freezing, or smoking. Histamine production occurs rapidly at high temperatures, but slows dramatically at temperatures below 40°F. Fish held at 90°F can become toxic within six hours and fish held at 70°F can become toxic within 24 hours.

Landing, Bleeding, and Chilling the Tuna

Like many other anglers, I have developed what works best for me when landing tuna, which is a combination of some of the methods listed below.

1. **Landing**. It's important to land the fish as quickly as possible once it's hooked. Prolonged struggle will result in higher body temperatures and reduced quality. This is where using a heavier leader or topshot can be a benefit because it helps you to land the fish quickly. I recommend fishing with the heaviest leader or topshot you can get away with. If you use a gaff, gaff the fish in the head or through the lower jaw, never in the body or you will destroy and contaminate the edible flesh. I prefer to gaff my fish using a 6-foot gaff and I just have to reach past the tuna when it swings close to the boat doing a death spiral, then pull the gaff to me, hopefully hooking the tuna in the head. Be careful with the gaff, however, as they can be very sharp. On one occasion, I lost a fish off the gaff and tried to gaff it again while it was flopping on the deck. I proceeded to run the tip of the gaff up along my calf and it was so sharp I didn't notice I was bleeding for a while. A quarter inch deeper and I would've had a serious issue offshore. Yet gaffs do tend to get dull after they've seen a lot of action and periodically they need to have their tip re-sharpened. Most of them have soft stainless steel hooks and it doesn't take much to sharpen one; I've sharpened them using a hook file a few times.

    Some guys prefer to use a big salmon net to land their fish and once the fish start doing death spirals, you only have to put the net in front of them on one of those spirals and they'll typically swim right in.

2. **Stunning**. Industry experts recommend stunning the fish immediately after you get it on deck to eliminate scale loss

and bruising. It's easier to stun the fish when it's still on the gaff or on the hook remover. Club the fish with a modified bat, mallet, or lead-filled steel pipe on the soft spot right above the eyes. Frankly, I rarely hear of anyone who does this. If people are going to take the time to do something, it's generally brain spiking to prevent the staccato drum roll (tail slapping the deck or the bleed bucket) that occurs many times after the fish has been landed.

3. **Brain Spiking**. Instead of, or immediately after stunning the fish, it can be immobilized by destroying its brain. (Spiking the brain is a required procedure for production of sashimi grade tuna worldwide.) In addition to immobilizing the fish, brain destruction helps stop the production of heat and acid, and the loss of energy rich compounds.

   To spike an albacore, position yourself so that you are balanced with the fish positioned on its belly, and the spiking tool (an ice pick or a sharpened screwdriver) firmly in one hand and the fish's tail in the other. Do not attempt spiking without complete control of your balance, the spiking tool, and the fish. Place the spike at the soft spot above the eyes at a 30-degree angle to the horizontal.

   Push the spike quickly into the skull maintaining the 30-degree angle while holding the tail with your other hand. Move the instrument from side to side to destroy the brain. The fish will shudder, all the muscles will flex, the mouth will open, and the pectoral fins will flue. If done properly, after one or two seconds, the fish will go limp.

   If not done properly, the fish can shudder violently creating the potential for personal injury, and further scale loss and bruising to the fish. With slippery conditions, this procedure can be a challenge, but after several attempts, brain destruction is swift and thorough.

4. **Bleeding**. Bleeding right away is very important to having a nice quality product once you get back to the dock. Bleeding improves the appearance of uncooked tuna loins and initially helps to reduce the fish temperature on deck. Fish should be bled for 10 to 15 minutes after stunning (brain spiking) and then immediately chilled. Bleeding is most efficient when done immediately after the fish is landed, and when the heart is left intact to take advantage of its pumping action. Bleeding can be accomplished in at least three ways; use the one easiest for you. If one cut does not produce blood, try one of the other methods. Usually one of the three methods mentioned below will get the job done but you could use more than one cut which may promote more efficient bleeding. If possible, orient the fish head down to help the fish bleed out easier once it is cut. If you're fortunate to get the bite wide open, do not let the blood run out of your bleed bucket and overboard or the sharks will show up sooner than you'll like. Some anglers who tend to troll will have an outlet on their bleed bucket which works great when catching fish on the troll, but when you're dead in the water working them over, you'll want to close or plug it to prevent the blood from running out. Once you're done fishing either in that location or you're done for the day, then dump the blood. If you have live bait onboard and plan to use them the next day, don't dump the bleed bucket unless you're moving through the water, otherwise the bait pump will suck up the bloody water into your bait tank. Too much blood in the bait tank will kill your bait from lack of oxygen.

Pectoral Cut: This cut is the most common in tuna fisheries worldwide. With the fish on its side, measure 1.5 to 2 inches (about the width of two fingers) from the base of (under) the pectoral fin along the midline. Make a shallow cut about ⅛ to ¼ inch wide and ¼ inch deep along the raised ridge near the midline using a clean, sharp knife with a narrow blade. If this cut is made too deep or too wide, usable flesh can be destroyed and reduce the fish's value. Flip the fish over and repeat the cut on the other side. This cut is very effective with albacore. I have used this method numerous times and there's no doubt about whether you found the vein as they spurt blood from this type of cut.

Gill Cut: The gill arch cut is the one most commonly used now in the U.S. albacore fishery and the cut I use 95% of the time. With the fish still on the gaff, lift the gill cover and sever the gill arch and insert the knife behind the gill through the gill membrane, and cut up toward the spine, severing the blood vessels at the top of the gills.

Throat or Nape Cut: This cut involves cutting the blood vessel between the heart and the gills. It can be done in either of two ways, depending on the preference of the buyer. With the fish on its back or side, cut the "V"-shaped nape between the gill covers and the body of the fish to the artery just below the surface. An alternative that leaves the head firmly attached to the body is to make a shallow cut just inside the point of the "V" of the nape; lift the artery with your finger and cut. The heart is about three inches behind or inside the point of the "V." Take care not to sever the heart or you will lose the pumping action the heart provides. Experienced albacore anglers have variations of this cut that they find faster for them. Again, keeping the fish on the gaff while making the cut helps to control the fish, especially if you're gaffing and cutting them without brain spiking or stunning them. When we have a wide open bite going I usually gaff, then cut them, before taking them off the gaff and placing them head down in my 30-gallon bleed bucket.

CHILLING

ALBACORE SHOULD BE CHILLED WITHIN 15–20 MINUTES OF LANDING to ensure you end up with a high quality product without histamine. As a general rule, one day of shelf life is lost for each hour an albacore is left on deck. This rate of decomposition is three times that of other fishes. This is where having someone act as the deck hand is important to make sure things happen in a timely manner or you're just wasting your time out there landing fish without taking the time to properly take care of them.

A good rule of thumb is 5 pounds of ice per tuna, although I would consider that a minimum. If you plan on catching 20 tuna, plan on 100 pounds of ice. Ice is cheap so don't skimp on something so important.

Some anglers prefer to use a slurry to bleed their fish and for the life of me I don't understand the logic of this. Have you ever had a bloody nose? What did you do to stop the bleeding—you put an ice pack on it. What do you think happens to a tuna with his heart still pumping out blood when you immerse them into a cold bath of ice water? They're going to slow down bleeding out and you run the risk of them not bleeding out properly. Yes, it's important to get them bled out immediately and then chilled all in a timely manner but I prefer to bleed them out in my bleed bucket (head down), then I place them into my fish boxes where I will use a slurry to chill them. I use one large handful of rock salt for every 100 quarts of fish storage, then add three to five bags of ice depending on size, and fill the rest with sea water. By the time you get back to the dock, you won't be able to put your hand in the slurry. If you're tired from all the action and plan to cark/filet the tuna yourself or just don't want to deal with them, leave them in the slurry till the next day and you'll find a solid layer of ice on the slurry when you open the fish boxes. The fish will be so cold you'll have a hard time hanging on to them but they will sure cark/filet nicely since the meat will be cold and firm.

Safety at Sea

I've been fishing offshore for more than 40 years and I'm never surprised at the things I see people do. They get so wrapped up in wanting to get offshore that they fail to equip their boat with the basic safety equipment needed to run 50 miles offshore. It's one thing to be just across the bar and fishing near the beach as most of the time there are other boats around should you get in trouble and need assistance. But it's another thing when you're 50 miles offshore, with no one around, and suddenly basic safety becomes much more important. The topic of safety at sea could be another book by itself but I'm only going to touch on the highlights of this very in-depth topic. It's not a sexy topic so no sense in boring you to tears.

I fish in the Columbia River in August when the Buoy 10 salmon fishery cranks up and there are days when it looks like you can just walk across the boats. One morning I came out of the channel in very thick fog, guiding my way out to the main river channel with the aid of my chart plotter and radar. As I slowly worked my way along, I noticed boats tied off to pilings waiting for the fog to lift or someone to follow. They didn't have a chart plotter or radar and many of them didn't even have a VHF.

Garmin 8212

Chartplotter - If you're planning to run offshore, two of the basic pieces of navigational equipment, at a minimum, would be a Chartplotter and a VHF radio. Chartplotters have come a long way in the last few years and many of them can be networked together or have the ability to add additional features, such as installing a transducer for sonar or adding a radar. If you're technically challenged, some chartplotters have features such as turning on the breadcrumb trail, which leaves you a trail to follow home at the end of the day. If it's foggy and you don't have radar, the breadcrumb trail will give you a little peace of mind that you're on the right path, provided you used a good route when leaving port.

VHF Marine Radio - A VHF marine radio is a combination transmitter/receiver and only operates on standard, international frequencies known as channels. Channel 16 is the international calling and distress channel. Transmission power ranges between 1 and 25 watts, giving a range of up to about 60 miles between antennas mounted on tall ships and 5 miles between antennas mounted on small boats. The signal is by direct line of sight, which is why the

Coast Guard mounts their antennas on tall hills on the edge of the coastline. It gives them the ability to pick up even a weak signal from a long distance.

VHF radios can be fix mounted or handheld portable units. A fixed mounted set generally has the advantages of a more reliable power source, higher transmitting power, a larger and more effective aerial, and a bigger display and buttons. A portable set (often essentially a waterproof, VHF walkie-talkie in design) can be carried on a person's body, has its own power source, and is waterproof if GMDSS-approved (Global Maritime Distress Safety System).

Digital Selective Calling equipment (DSC) is a part of the Global Maritime Distress Safety System. A radio with this feature will have a DSC button which automatically sends a digital distress signal identifying the calling vessel using a telephone-type number known as Maritime Mobile Service Identity (MMSI). If connected to a GPS receiver, it will also give the distressed vessel's position.

Radar - The chartplotter is great for navigation but one of the features it lacks is the ability to show you what's ahead in the fog. I have a friend who was running offshore out of Newport, Oregon, headed for the chicken ranch for a day of halibut fishing. They were about 10 miles offshore when they noticed something dark in the fog and slowed down just in time to watch a large barge pass by them only a few yards away. If they had been just 20–30 seconds earlier, they might have passed in between the tug and barge and gotten tangled or even rolled by the towing hawser (cable). It scared him enough to go back to port and within days, had added radar to his system. If you have radar, you should use it on bluebird days just to get used to what things look like so you're more comfortable when navigating in the fog or dark. I've had days where I was in fog all the way offshore to the tuna grounds and all the way home.

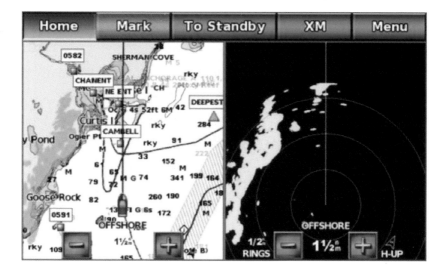

Garmin 740xs

AIS - Another fairly inexpensive device to add to your chartplotter is an AIS receiver or a unit that transmits your information as well as receives that of other marine traffic. Check your chartplotter to see if it has the ability to add the feature. What is AIS? As defined by the Coast Guard Code of Federal Regulations CFR's - Per 33 CFR § 164.46, Automatic Identification System, or AIS, provides vessel information, including the vessel's identity, type, position, course, and speed.

This is also a great safety device when fishing Buoy 10 since it will show the large vessels coming and going out of the Columbia River. They show up on the chartplotter and you can watch them moving along giving you time to get out of their way. If you and your buddies each have it, it's a great way to see where each of you is fishing. If one of you gets a hot bite going, you can tell your other buddies without broadcasting your location over the VHF since they can see you on their chartplotter screen.

Fuel Capacity - On one trip a few years back I was running offshore on a sporty ocean when I heard a couple of guys talking on the VHF radio and one of the boats needed to stop to re-adjust his metal gas cans that he had strapped inside the open bow. I turned the volume up to see if I was hearing things right. The only thing that this guy was doing right was that he had a buddy boat. At least someone would be around to witness the fireball when the cans came loose when one bounced against another causing his trip to come to an abrupt and explosive ending. The first thing that comes to mind is that his boat doesn't have the fuel range to be running for tuna. The basic rule of thumb to consider should be that you need a minimum capacity of 1/3 of the fuel to make it to the tuna grounds, and another 1/3 to make it back home safely. The remaining 1/3 is in reserve in the event the ocean gets big and now the boat is loaded not just with the ice you brought with you, but also with the fish you caught and it's taking much longer to get back. I've been offshore on a few occasions when the ocean swell and wind direction had changed and now couldn't run straight back to the port but had to run straight east for 10 miles then turn to port, taking a different angle on the waves. It's easier to quarter the waves than it is to pound straight into them.

I was one of those guys who thought I was pretty safe but now I know I've been very fortunate over the years. But I learned a big lesson a few years back. I was in Southern California fishing a shark tournament out of Dana Point and we had been experiencing beautiful flat seas. The ocean was great—unfortunately the fishing wasn't—and as the last day was winding down, we found ourselves a few miles outside the bay near Avalon on Catalina Island. We decided to end the day and run into Avalon to pick up some fuel. We stopped at the fuel dock and struggled to get fuel to flow into the fuel fill, which I later learned was a flaw in the fuel system on that particular boat. After 40 minutes, I was able to get it to take about five gallons and had some concern about making it all the way across the channel on the return trip. As we untied the lines on the dock, a boat came into the harbor mentioning how nasty it was offshore. We shrugged and thought, "No way!" It was greasy flat when we came in just a few minutes earlier but in the 40 minutes we had been in the harbor, the wind and swells had picked up and it was a whole new ocean and not a very pretty one at that. I've never seen it change that much in such a short period of time. We had eight-foot swells with two-foot wind waves.

The seas had been so nice earlier that we had the top completely down on the boat but now it was clear we needed some protection from the sea spray. We stopped just long enough to put the top back up, as well as all the side curtains. We dumped all the remaining chum that we had onboard in an effort to lighten the load and before we started across the channel, we all put our lifejackets on.

Down the swell we'd go, plowing into the trough and powering back up the other side. It was a constant job running the throttle. As we raced down the swell, I needed to give it a little throttle as we neared the bottom causing the bow to rise slightly so we'd glide up the backside of the swell. Too late on the throttle and we'd plow the trough sending a wall of water over the top almost broaching the boat. Too much throttle as we came over the top of the swell and we'd go airborne landing in the bottom of the next trough. It was 45 minutes of white knuckle running that I would never want to do again. We made it safely back to Dana Point arriving on fumes with just enough fuel to get the boat back on the trailer. I did not have the experience or the knowledge of what my proper needs were for the body of water we were fishing and we were fortunate we never lost power as we would've been swamped within minutes.

That was many years ago and I've since taken the time to learn what is needed when I step onto a boat under any circumstance. I'm sure there are a lot of others out there who think they're safe partly because they haven't had an incident to raise their awareness.

Offshore safety is not the sexiest of topics, especially when you'd rather be playing with lures or something that might catch a fish. But I would encourage anyone who has the opportunity to take a Coast Guard auxiliary course if you get the chance, or even better yet, go through the Coast Guard Masters course. A number of years back I was running charters, which required a Coast Guard license, so I enrolled in a course and was humbled at how little I really knew. I haven't run charters for the last six years, but I still maintain my 100 Ton Coast Guard Masters license.

To Go or Not to Go - One of the things people need to learn is how to determine when to go and when to stay tied to the dock. Some of that equation is based on how comfortable you are in running in the forecasted seas and knowing if you have the skills if things get worse. It is very important for the skippers of their boats to develop an attitude that they have the final word on going or staying. Too many times I've seen situations where their buddies coaxed the skippers into going. Then they get offshore and they're anxious because they're nervous about whether they made a mistake and they aren't sure what they'll do if the ocean gets worse. Developing a system of how to interpret the forecast is a good start to being safe and confident in the ocean. The NOAA (National Oceanic and Atmospheric Administration) forecasts are based upon information that is plugged into a model and then spits out its forecast. But many times it's not that accurate, whereas I use a couple of web-based forecasting services in addition to NOAA such as Magic Seaweed and Wetsand. Sites designed for surfers use the same information that NOAA does, but instead of being plugged into a model, the information is interpreted for their customers. I learned from my Dana Point shark tournament experience not to just rely on NOAA. It pays to use a number of sources for your information, then compare them to see who's the most accurate on a consistent basis.

When you're offshore fishing, take the time to observe the conditions. Then if you have the capability to check the buoy while offshore, see what it's reading for current conditions. Many of today's chartplotters have a feature to add a weather subscription available through Sirius XM which will give you weather forecasts as well as the ability to click on the closest buoy. If you don't have that ability, once you are back in port, go online and check the buoy to see what actual conditions were while you were out there. You'll soon develop a feel for what conditions will be like based on different forecasts. Browse the NOAA website to find the closest buoy in your area. Some anglers will still load up and run a few miles offshore to put the hairy eyeball on it just for their own satisfaction. I have to admit I've done that a few times and in most instances, turned around and came back into port. Pushing your luck on a sporty ocean is never worth it. Besides, if you pound your way out to the tuna grounds, fishing is generally not very good. There are always exceptions, but it's rare to get many fish when the seas are big.

Bar Crossings - One of the most dangerous things you can do is cross a bar during hazardous conditions. A bar crossing is that point where a river meets the ocean and in the Northwest, there are a few treacherous ones. The Columbia River Bar is known as the Graveyard of the Pacific and rightfully so. It's five miles across and when navigating the crossing, you're in the bar crossing for a couple of miles, depending on whether you cut to the north or south to get out of the flow. . On any given day and depending on the ocean conditions, one area where you cross might have better conditions than another area of the bar. I learned to cross the Columbia River Bar by a local charter skipper who taught me a lot about the ebb and flow of the crossing that makes it so dangerous. I didn't learn it overnight, either. It took quite a few crossings with him to see different scenarios and learn how much it can truly change from day to day. It's very important to learn when and where to cross. It's also just as important to learn when *not* to attempt a crossing. I've run a boat out of almost every port in Washington and Oregon and there are a lot of differences among the many bar crossings. Where the Chetco River meets the ocean in Brookings, the river just opens up into the sea and there is no bar crossing for the most part—a big difference from the Columbia River. The Columbia River Bar Crossing is very intimidating for those not familiar with it, but with some study and educating yourself about it, you can learn when and where to navigate it while building confidence on every trip.

Where to cross a bar can change from season to season due to big storms that push sand into areas creating shoaling or shallow areas where waves could break and possibly capsize a boat. I've been offshore when the bar conditions deteriorated to the point that the Coast Guard closed the bar to all recreational traffic until conditions improved. Most of the time you just have to wait for the tide to change and the bar hopefully will settle down, allowing you to cross it safely.

The best time to cross the bar is when the tide is flooding or coming in. The worst time to cross is when it's ebbing or flowing out. Three hours before low tide is known as "maximum ebb," when the outflow is running the strongest, which can create the worst conditions on the bar.

There are two high tides and two low tides every 24 hours, which are also affected by the moon. NOAA defines tides as very long waves that move across the oceans. They are caused by gravitational forces exerted upon the earth by the moon, and to a lesser extent, the sun. When the highest point in the wave reaches a coast, the coast experiences a high tide. As the earth spins, different areas of earth face the moon, and this rotation causes the tides to cycle every six hours as the earth rotates.

If you're planning a day of fishing offshore, you'll want to look for the best time and best conditions to cross the bar in the morning when going out, and then again when coming back in the afternoon. A typical scenario might be crossing the bar in the morning during a flood tide, which is an incoming or rising tide, fishing most of the day, and timing your return to coincide with another flood tide. Keep in mind that the tide changes every six hours. If you don't have a flood tide in the morning when you want to leave, you might want to delay your departure until the tide changes.

Some of the worst conditions are when there is a minus ebb tide and the ocean has a pretty good-sized swell. However, if the tide is ebbing or flowing out and the ocean is flat, many times the bar can be nice. The size of the offshore swell can make a big difference as to what conditions might be like when you're crossing the bar.

If you're coming out of the harbor, many times you can call on the VHF to see if anyone has recently crossed the bar and is willing to give you a first-hand report of what it was like. Most of the fleet of recreational anglers have a VHF channel that they monitor in each port. If you can't raise anyone, you can also call the Coast Guard on VHF Channel 22 for their most recent bar report. They say they change their report as needed when bar conditions change, but I can tell you from experience that that isn't always the case, although they are pretty good about keeping up on things. I was in Winchester Bay, southwest of Eugene, Oregon, quite a few years back, and the bite was extremely slow in the river, so my buddies and I decided to run out to the ocean. I called the Coast Guard for a bar report which indicated the bar should be very nice. But when we rounded the corner and headed up through the channel, 20-foot breakers were coming across the bar and we had 4-foot wind chop pounding us. Needless to say, I called them back and gave them my firsthand report, prompting them to close the bar crossing. The Coast Guard appreciates the feedback we give them and in some cases, we are their eyes on the water.

I use a web-based tide chart service, www.saltwatertides.com, for planning my trips offshore. I also use a number of web-based weather services to see how big the swells are predicted to be, which can also help me to determine what bar crossing conditions might be like.

Life Jackets - One of the rules on my boat is that you have to wear a life jacket while we're running in or out of port to the fishing grounds. Doesn't matter if we're salmon fishing just a few miles out of port or tuna fishing 50 miles offshore. Things can happen very fast and coming to an abrupt stop while also trying to put on a life jacket can be very challenging at the least. It's a rule I live by and everyone has to follow it or they stay on the dock.

A few years back we were filming an episode with Tred Barta and had Danny Kirsic, one of the cameramen, onboard. We were

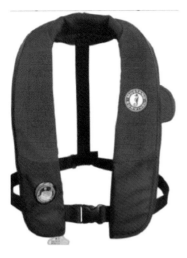
Mustang Auto Inflatable PFD

about to pull away from the dock when we handed out inflatable Mustang PFDs (Personal Flotation Devices) and Danny mentioned he never wore one. He gave me a funny look when I told him he'd have to wear it as it's a boat rule. Danny's an easygoing guy and after a few minutes of helping others get their PFDs adjusted properly, I turned back to look at him. He was wearing his life jacket and he was hoisting a video camera up onto his shoulder to see if the PFD was going to give him problems. He was good to go and never took it off all day. After a day of fishing and filming, we pulled back into the slip just as Tred Barta came along the dock and asked him what he was doing wearing a life jacket. "He made me wear it!" Danny said, and I grinned. I don't have a problem if the ocean is flat and people want to take off their life jacket once we get to where we're fishing, but it has to be close by should they need it in a hurry. I've had days offshore when it was pretty sporty and the crew never took off their life jackets, wearing them all day. The inflatable PFDs are generally pretty comfortable and don't usually get in the way of fishing.

If you're in the market for an inflatable PFD for fishing, you'll want to consider where you'll wear it. For example, do you fish in an environment that is damp or foggy? If so, you'll want an auto inflatable hydrostatic release PFD versus the ones that use a tablet that dissolves to activate the inflation of the vest. Those tablets have a tendency to dissolve after the PFDs have been worn in rain or foggy, damp weather and the last thing you need is for the vest to automatically inflate while you're fishing. There are many manufacturers of life jackets out there, but the bottom line is, if it's bulky

and restricts your mobility, you probably won't wear it as often as you might if it was nice and comfortable.

EPIRB - An Emergency Position Indicating Radio Beacon or EPIRB is used to alert search and rescue services in the event of an emergency. It does this by transmitting a coded message on the 406 MHz distress frequency via satellite and earth stations to the nearest rescue coordination center. EPIRBs are commonly mounted on boats and can be activated with a hydrostatic release when the boat sinks or they can be manually activated. EPIRBs work with the COSPAS-SARSAT polar orbiting satellite system, giving true global coverage. There is an alert delay of about 45 minutes dependent on when the satellites come into view on the horizon.

Category I EPIRBs rely on satellite and can determine the position of your EPIRB to within three miles. The coded message identifies the exact vessel to which the EPIRB is registered. This information allows the rescue services to eliminate false alerts and launch an appropriate rescue. Category II are GPS-enabled EPIRBs and have a built-in transmitter which will typically alert the rescue services within three minutes, to a positional accuracy of +/- 50 meters, and they update every 20 minutes.

THE DIFFERENCES BETWEEN EPIRBS AND PLBS

PERSONAL LOCATION BEACONS - PLBs WORK IN EXACTLY THE SAME way as EPIRBs—by sending a coded message on the 406 MHz distress frequency which is relayed via the COSPAS-SARSAT global satellite system.

However, there are a number of differences between them. PLBs are designed to be carried on the person so they are much smaller; some are not much larger than the size of a mobile phone. PLBs are designed to be used anywhere in the world, on the sea and on land. Some don't float but may come with an additional flotation sleeve which they should be carried in. PLBs, once activated, will transmit for a minimum of 24 hours, while the battery life on an EPIRB is at least double (a minimum of 48 hours). An EPIRB is registered to a vessel, whereas a PLB is registered to a person. There is no cost to register them. This means that if you are crewing a vessel and you switch to a new vessel, the PLB is still correctly registered; however, if you have an EPIRB and buy a new boat, you will need to re-register it when installing it in your new boat. There is no cost to register them but if you neglect registering it and you activate it in an emergency it will delay any attempt at a rescue while authorities try to determine if it is a real emergency.

A basic EPIRB could cost as little as $600; one with GPS built-in, a bit more. A PLB is generally about $250 depending on the brand. After purchasing, there is no extra cost involved, apart from the cost of replacing the battery. Unlike other rescue location products, there is no subscription cost for using the tracking system.

Most EPIRBS are fitted with a battery which should last a minimum of five years if the unit is unused. Most EPIRBS require the unit to be sent back to the supplier or the manufacturer for the battery to be replaced. The batteries are of special use type intended to last a minimum of five years and it's not uncommon for one to cost $250.

Flares - Flares are a requirement for anyone boating and you'll want to familiarize yourself with what's required when venturing offshore. There's also quite a difference among various types of flares. Flares and other safety devices carry different ratings. A SOLAS rating (Safety Of Life At Sea) typically indicates the safety standard the device meets.

SOLAS parachute flares use a rocket propellant to send them skyward up to an elevation of 1,000 feet, and they then descend slowly, burning for more than 30 seconds. Meteor flares use a small gun-like device to shoot them up to 300 feet and they burn for less than 10 seconds. Most parachute flares are SOLAS rated whereas meteor flares are not. SOLAS parachute flares will typically cost $45–$55 each versus $30 for a small four-pack of non-SOLAS rated aerial flares.

When you're 50 miles offshore and your life is on the line, having a flare that can shoot 1,000 feet into the air and burn for almost a minute might be what saves your life. Look at it this way, the difference between a gun style aerial flare and a SOLAS parachute flare is that one is a pop gun and the other is a howitzer. However, because of this power, keep in mind that parachute flares are dangerous and you should learn the proper technique for shooting them.

It's a good idea to also have handheld flares on board and like parachute flares, they also come SOLAS or non-SOLAS rated.

It's important to regularly check your flares since they have an expiration date. If you have a flare that has expired, you can keep it onboard but it needs to be in a separate container from your other flares and you should label the container in big letters, "EXPIRED." This hopefully will prevent someone from grabbing one of the expired flares in the event of an emergency. I keep my expired flares in a box at home and it's a good idea to use them for practice during 4th of July celebrations or at organized planned safety practices, which need to be approved by the Coast Guard.

If you have an emergency offshore during the daylight hours, parachute flares are great, but it's also a good idea to have a smoke flare that can pinpoint your location. Most smoke flares are SOLAS rated and will float if needed.

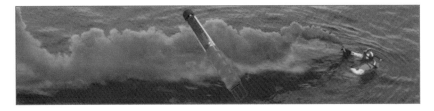

It's best to keep all your flares in a waterproof container. I keep all mine in a waterproof ditch bag which also has other items as well. Sometimes if I fish on another boat and don't know what they have for safety equipment or suspect they might not be as well-equipped, I take my own ditch bag just to be safe.

Ditch Bag - All boaters and anglers should have some type of waterproof container/ditch bag onboard to carry their safety gear such as flares. I also keep a handheld GPS, handheld VHF, EPIRB, first aid kit, whistle, flashlight, mirror, and satellite phone in my ditch bag.

Safety Talk - When I'm running offshore, my ditch bag is brought up out of my console and placed under the portside helm seat. It's always placed in the same position and is readily available in the event we should have an emergency. My wife is normally fishing with me and when we have guests onboard, I do a safety talk where I also assign tasks in the event of an emergency. It's her responsibility to take the ditch bag if we have to abandon the boat. The safety talk is something everyone should do prior to every trip so everyone onboard knows what safety equipment is available and where it is located. Get in the habit of doing it even if you're just fishing for salmon close to shore.

Life Raft - If you have the space, it's a good idea to have a life raft. There are a number of manufacturers who make a six-man life raft that's affordable for small boats. I have a Coastal Commander six-man life raft made by Revere which sells for $1,500 to $1,700, depending on where you find it. They are available in a valise bag or in a hard, watertight canister. The hard, watertight canister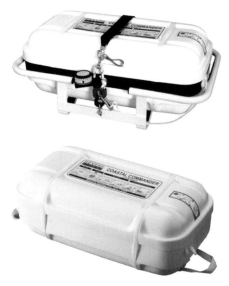

type also has a metal cradle and hydrostatic release available. The hydrostatic release will activate when the boat sinks and the raft will float to the surface. I chose to buy mine in the canister but in many situations, you have time to deploy the raft and if that situation ever presents itself, I'd prefer to deploy the raft and climb in without having to go in the water.

The raft is equipped with additional safety equipment such as flares, first aid kit, floating knife, and mirror. These are many of the things you'd find in most ditch bags and you can specify the things you'd like to have them add when ordering your raft.

Rafts also have an expiration date tag or sticker and have to be repacked every few years. It varies from manufacturer as to how many years they're good between repacking. Mine is repacked and recertified every three years. When they repack them, they will open and activate the raft to check for holes or leaks, and check and replace flares as well as any other safety device with an expiration date.

Having a life raft, EPIRB, SOLAS flares, handheld VHF, and the other safety devices I carry, gives me peace of mind in the event we ever have an emergency offshore and have to abandon ship. I would anticipate and hope we'd not be in the raft or water very long before being rescued. I like to prepare for the worst scenario and hope for the best outcome.

Catching Fish on Those Tough Days

Every year as I prepare for the sport show season I like to add a little fresh content to my seminars, and one of the things I like to do is ask people what they would like to learn more about in those seminars. After over 20 years of chasing albacore off the Oregon Coast, I've learned that each season is a little different than the year before and this past season was another year of surprises. Oregon and Washington's albacore fishery is still pretty much a new fishery for most offshore anglers and if you don't subscribe to being a student of the fishery, you could suffer some long days with little to show for the effort. This year the one question that came up the most was, "Could you please give a seminar on how to catch fish on those tough days?" That left me thinking about what I do on those days.

There are a couple of things I firmly believe—first and foremost you need to learn how to find the fish. I don't mean casually learn to find fish but get really good at it. The other key factor is you need to learn a couple of methods of catching tuna. The trolling game can work fine most of the time in the early season. But what happens when the fish decide to throw you a curve and you troll all day, returning to port with only a couple of fish in the box or worse yet, you get blanked after running 50 miles offshore? Don't get me wrong. I certainly have been in that boat a time or two, although thankfully, it's been a while since the last time that's happened.

The successful anglers who bring good numbers of fish back

time after time have all learned that one arrow in the quiver really limits your opportunities. Whereas those who take the time to learn new techniques generally fair better than those who live and die by the troll show or those who only know how to fish live bait.

Some of the best tuna anglers I know fish out of ports with no live bait available and at times don't care even if it is available. They have learned how to adjust based on the conditions they are handed.

I truly believe that if you learn three basic techniques and have the proper equipment for each, you will catch fish on most days. Obviously, learning sound troll techniques including a few variations to the troll, is one of those three methods. Learning to fish swimbaits—either on the troll or running and gunning casting swimbaits to jumpers—is also a fun and effective method. The third technique that requires a little more investment is learning to work the iron. The rods, reels, and gear are very specific to making this technique work properly and if you buy into doing it right, this can prove to be one of the most important arrows in your quiver that can make a slow day turn into a good day. I doubt you'll find a faster way to plug the boat than with a couple of anglers who know how to work iron effectively. The technique is not that hard to learn but it requires a little investment in the proper gear. Parabolic rods designed to load properly, paired up with high speed 6:1 reels, along with a collection of jigs, and it's game on!

Although none of these techniques will be effective if you don't back up and think about one of the most basic steps—how to find the fish. Because if you're not in an area that has fish, you are definitely at a handicap! I use a web-based sea surface website such as Terrafin to look for defined temperature breaks with temperatures at or above 58 degrees. I then look to see if the chlorophyll charts overlay and match up those temperature breaks. The third thing to consider is to see if these temperature breaks and high chlorophyll count areas are known to produce fish. The ocean is no different than a great steelhead stream in that there are areas where fish are known to congregate such as steelhead holding in a tail out on a stream. The ocean is the offshore version of the same thing. It has contours from underwater canyons and sea mounds that produce upwellings where bait gets pushed to the surface by currents. These currents also tend to keep and contain the bait in certain areas— areas where tuna will also congregate. It pays to spend a little time to research these areas online before burning a couple hundred dollars in fuel running all over the ocean without any starting point other than a hunch. If the sea surface temperature websites don't have a recent satellite picture due to heavy cloud cover, then I like to start by going back to places where I've caught fish before or places historically known to produce fish.

There are a couple of things I would caution you about. Don't chase "radio fish" as that rarely seems to produce very many fish, and don't fish where there are a lot of boats. "Radio fish" is when you hear various anglers on the VHF radio reference they've caught a fish and you decide to move to their location or attempt to find their location. The prop wash from numerous boats in one area will also sometimes drive the fish down. If you are constantly having to turn to avoid other boats, there are too many boats in your area. Yes, there's peace of mind having other boats around in the event you have a problem, but that doesn't mean you still can't move a few miles to find fish not being worked over by the whole fleet.

On one offshore trip, I went to where a bite had been reported the prior day and trolled among a fleet of boats that only produced good radio chatter. Two hours spent there, including changing gear and techniques a couple of times with nothing in the box to show for it, was enough for me. I told the crew to pull the gear and we left for greener pastures. We left the flotilla and ran 20 miles to a location where I'd caught fish three days earlier. We only had the gear back in the water for less than a minute when we started catching fish. We fished the rest of the day by ourselves with no boat in sight for hours and came home with a nice load of fish, unlike most of those who chose to stay where we had first started our day.

The summer of 2013 was a season where the tuna were not on

the surface most of the time and left trolling anglers frustrated and many times, empty handed. It didn't matter if they left port with a live well full of anchovies because many use the troll to find fish rather than other methods of finding fish.

On another trip, I took a friend and two 12-year-old boys to introduce them to the addiction that consumes us blue water guys. We passed an incredible armada of boats on the run offshore only to find a floating parking lot of well over 100 boats 50 miles offshore. When I pulled throttles back and settled into the water, I noticed the tuna were under the boat, but down 30–50 feet. I had been listening to the radio on the run out and heard that the troll anglers were struggling to catch a fish. I could see why as the tuna were too far down to come up for most troll gear. We didn't even get the troll gear out but instead chose to throw a couple of good handfuls of chum, while one of my fishing buddies dropped the iron down to them, and my wife deployed a couple of swimbait rods to drift along. We then put a couple of live baits overboard and waited.

It only took a couple of attempts with the iron before we started hooking up and soon we had the bite wide open. Once that happened, everything in the water was catching fish. We drifted for a couple of hours, eventually hooking over 50 fish and soon had a worn-out crew.

We drifted most of the morning watching one boat after another troll by and at times coming within 50 yards of us causing our bite to die off and sound the fish sending them down. But we would just drop the iron back down, hook them up, and start bringing the school back up. That had to be frustrating for the others to watch as we landed fish after fish while they trolled in vain.

This is where learning to use more than one method to find fish and then another method to catch them, paid off. We recognized the fish were under the boat, but were down a fair distance. But we didn't even hesitate, having the confidence to know that we could get them with iron along with a little chumming to bring them up. I have to admit that having a Garmin CHIRP sonar and set to only 100 feet or less, definitely helps to find fish and can be a game changer some days.

The one buddy who was fishing with me swears he hasn't seen me troll for fish very much the last few times he's been on my boat. That summer was a season where the anglers who knew how to find fish and knew how to work iron had a great season and in many instances, out-fished even those with live bait.

I keep telling people it's not that hard to catch tuna, although that summer it was definitely a little tougher than in years past, especially if you only had one arrow in your quiver. Learn the basics, hone your skills, and add a few new techniques to your game plan, and you'll improve your odds on those tough days when Charlie decides to be a little finicky.

Here are a few tips on how to catch fish on those tough days:

- Go back to where you've historically caught fish and remember to keep a log of where you catch your fish
- Check the sea surface temps/chlorophyll shots
- Do not run to radio fish—develop your own style and think it through
- Remember the basics—birds, jumpers, temperature breaks, etc., but be willing to think outside the box—Confidence is your friend
- Pay attention to the little things—boat attitude, fishing style, working as a team
- Use a combination of techniques—trolling, swimbaits, small baits, etc.
- Drop down to small lures under four inches with troll gear
- Keep your spread together but possibly farther back than normal—play with the distance. Try it short, such as 10–15 feet, as well as way back at 75 feet+
- Try diving lures such as Rapala's and divers with small lures
- Troll swimbaits with fluorocarbon leaders
- Forget trying to get multiple hookups by continuing to troll after getting hooked up

- Use chum after a hookup and possible dead baits/chum on a live bait hook using an inline sinker four feet ahead of the bait, then troll slowly
- Don't be impatient to leave after a hookup—work it a little
- Keep your head up and stay positive, you are going to catch fish—don't just give in and troll all over the ocean

Fishing Smart

From time to time we need to be reminded of the mistakes we've made and hopefully over the years, we'll need less reminding. It pays to pay attention and be a smart angler. There've been a few times I've shaken my head at people who get caught up in what everyone else is doing and don't take the time to really think about what they're hearing when they get a report and to modify their actions if necessary.

On one trip, there had been one report after another all week to indicate the bite wasn't very good until after lunch so those reports prompted me to delay our departure the next morning. We went for breakfast, then left the dock around 10 a.m., running 35 miles offshore to find a fleet of unhappy and very disappointed fishermen working the area with not much to show for their time and effort.

I had informed my crew not to expect too much till the afternoon. We arrived on the tuna grounds around 11 a.m. and were picking off a fish periodically. By late afternoon we only had six fish and my crew was now starting to wonder if it was going to happen for us. Most of the fleet had left the dock early that morning and by 2 p.m. were thoroughly frustrated; some of them only catching one or two fish before throwing in the towel and heading for home, their tail between their legs, leaving only a couple of us to work the area. Then it happened—the bite came on and in the next two hours, we put another 35 fish in the fish boxes. We left them still chewing the paint off the bottom of the boat but my crew was worn-out and had all the fish they wanted. The other two boats around us also got in on the action and were still hammering them when we left for home.

I don't mind getting up early but it amazes me that people think you have to leave the dock at o'dark thirty every time. Some of the best days I've had were days I left after everyone else was long gone.

Running to the blue water is another big sin. I can't count how many times I've seen and heard of anglers running to the blue water to find tuna only to run right past birds, warm water breaks, and other signs indicating potential fish miles way inside of where the reports of fish had been coming from. I have been guilty of this although not as much the last few years. On November 9th, 2014, I decided to venture offshore and see if the fish were still out there. The water was still plenty warm and a good forecast made things ideal to take a peek. It had been a few weeks since the last trip and the tuna were 40 miles out during the October trips. Fishing for tuna in November is unheard of in the Northwest but the boat was still in my slip at the coast, so why not? We picked up bait and ran offshore, headed to the spot where a few weeks earlier I had hammered them.

However, barely 20 miles offshore, we noticed a lot of birds and briefly watched to see what they were doing, but then we kept right on going. The water was warm enough but we never really saw a good temperature break on our instruments or any other signs besides the birds.

I was not expecting to find fish barely 20 miles from the beach and in fact, drove right past them thinking I would most likely find them somewhere near where we'd been catching them weeks before. I totally disregarded the obvious sign of birds working the water by having my mind set on the tuna being out there farther, although I was also not expecting 60 degree water that close to shore. This is where I made a big mistake that day as we should've stopped to take a look.

But we ran right past them, arrived at our location, and worked the general area for a couple of hours with nothing to show for our efforts. There were only four boats out there that day and we were all having pretty much the same luck.

After a few hours of no action and the thought of those birds in the back of my mind, I decided to run back inside to check them out. Could've done that on the way out, but I discounted the birds because I was so sure we'd be rewarded with more in a location that had proved to be a nice honey hole all season.

It didn't take long to run 20 miles back inside looking for the birds. And as luck would have it, once we found the birds, we saw jumpers. There was tuna jumping in every direction we looked.

The lesson is simple—if you find the telltale signs of tuna, stop and check it out. Too many people hear or read reports all week long of fish being caught in one area or another and put blinders on when headed offshore, running right over productive grounds and past blatant signs of life. They fail to realize that the fish haven't read those reports, that they possess tails, and that there are no pens holding them in one spot. If you find the fish, you are 50% there. Now you only have to worry about hooking and landing them.

Seven Deadly Sins of Albacore

Sloth, Pride, Lust, Envy, Greed, Gluttony, and Wrath. The history of this list most likely predates the Bible.

Even though the Bible proscribes all seven, this list is not strictly biblical. Nor is it Christian, as it transcends most religions in one form or another. According to most philosophers and theologians, if one or more of these doesn't seem like a big sin to you, you have already rationalized it. Don't despair, this book is about tuna fishing and not some sermon from the mount. But after researching topics and thinking about what I've learned these past 20 years, I was reminded of seven of the biggest transgressions made by offshore crews. We all have a few things in our past we'd like to bury and not revisit, but those things, when put in the proper perspective, are what builds character and makes us strong. They may be experiences we'd all like to forget, but sometimes the lessons learned prove invaluable later in life.

I grew up second in the pecking order and Mom always made sure we were all properly dressed for Sunday church. And if that wasn't enough, she had us in Bible school during the summers. Did I mention we were little hellions? I'm sure she probably thought we needed all the help we could get.

This chapter and subject was the topic of an article written by my friend Adam LaRossa a number of years ago and I recently ran across it again. When I took the time to read it once more and reflect about some of the mistakes made in life, I thought it was worth sharing and with Adam's blessing, have adapted it to my own personal experiences as well as others I have seen. While some of us avoid some of these sins when fishing offshore, every one of us—including my crew and myself—have all been guilty of one of these offenses at one time or another.

SLOTH is probably better known as laziness and is more accurately interpreted as apathy. When people are apathetic, they no longer really care about their duty, causing them to ignore their well-being.

Preparing your boat and gear to run 50 miles offshore is a time-consuming endeavor that cannot be ignored. It should begin long before the warm water forms and the first albacore show up. Laziness, probably more than anything else, leads to putting off or overlooking some of the items that factor into having a successful trip. This does not just include rods, reels, and lures, but more importantly, your boat and safety equipment.

There are no excuses for cutting corners on the maintenance of your boat when it comes to seaworthiness and the safety of your crew. You may get away with being lazy when you fish within a few miles of shore, but when you're 50 miles offshore, being able to run back in quickly or having the Coast Guard respond within minutes of a distress call is not an option.

Additionally, you'll likely find yourself running in the fog just as often as bright sunshine, so you better bring your A-game every time. Maintaining a meticulous boat with safety equipment that's up to date is a must when you're fishing in waters where help is hours away.

Offseason is the time for major work on the boat, giving you ample time to test new equipment or learn new electronics. You need to be comfortable with the electronics long before you subject yourself to running 20–30 miles through thick fog that is often found during the prime part of the season in August and September.

Then before every trip, take a few minutes to make sure things are working properly. Even on back-to-back trips, make sure things are still intact. Things tend to bounce loose from time to time, and running across a sporty ocean is not the best time to find something has come undone or is dangerously swinging back and forth.

Safety equipment is one of those things that often gets overlooked. It's definitely not a sexy topic and anglers tend to put it on the back burner for later. Life rafts are required to be repacked every couple of years and in many cases, have to be sent out for this service, which can take weeks or months. Waiting to the last minute to get this taken care of is apathy at its finest.

Now that you have the boat in order, it's time to devote your attention to your gear. Many times I've seen folks so excited to hear of the first fish being caught that they can't wait to get offshore into a hot bite. So they run offshore with their rods, reels, and lures in the same shape as when they ended the previous season. In some cases, anglers are too cheap to spring for new line and end up breaking off one fish after another.

Line is the weakest link you'll be attaching your hook– and hopefully your new fortunes—to. So wouldn't it make sense to check it? I check and replace fluorocarbon leaders on iron and live bait rods, in some cases, after every trip. Yes, it's expensive, but not as much as the $600 worth of fuel that it takes to run out to the tuna grounds only to break the fish off and then have little to show for all the effort because of being so cheap. At the very least, pull 50–100 feet off the reel and check it for nicks or frays.

PRIDE, simply put, is excessive belief in your own abilities. It's also about competition with others and failing to give them credit. According to scholars, if someone else's pride bothers you, that means you are guilty of pride. Failing to adapt to current methods that are producing the best results due to one's own excessive pride has resulted in many accomplished anglers going down in flames and losing their reputations. The fact is, methods that once worked may no longer produce as effectively as something new.

In the early years off the coast of the Northwest, the troll show was the only game in town. Trolling all day in hopes of hooking doubles, triples, quads, or even more was what everyone prescribed to. Then when you got into the late season and they were jumping but wouldn't bite, you just hung it up for the season. Those willing to adapt, soon learned how to troll swimbaits, while others learned the run and gun techniques. Those refusing to adapt mumbled about how great fishing used to be, while they watched others unload great catches at the docks, and later read about it in online chat forums. I was initially one of those guys who trolled around to no avail, while a few others were loading their boats and fine tuning their new techniques. But I wasted no time in swallowing my pride and soon learned some new tricks.

Then during the mid-2000s, Shimano re-introduced the Butterfly Jig system. My pride was no longer a factor and I quickly acquired the gear and knowledge to make this new system work for me. If there's one thing I've learned, it's that as much as we might like things to stay the same, they are constantly changing. One of the best things you can do is develop a network of buddies who are willing to share information and techniques and then you need to be willing to try something new.

In the last couple of seasons, I have seen pride plague many anglers as I've watched their boats troll constantly by while I sit dead in the water and my crew catches one fish after another for hours. I have given one seminar after another and some people just can't swallow their pride enough to show up at the seminars. Some of the best anglers I know are sometimes sitting in the seminar, which is one of the reasons they're so good at adapting to something new. In some of those seminars, I'm not the best angler in the room—I'm just someone willing to share what I've learned. Beginners filled with enthusiasm as well as seasoned veterans with many years under their belts all have experiences they are willing to share and those who listen and keep an open mind will tend to be the ones smiling after a day on the water when things are tough.

Another area where pride rears its ugly head is when guys think women don't know how to fish. The two ladies on my crew have grown used to hearing "Do you fish?" It doesn't even matter if the ladies are wearing one of our team tournament jerseys. I often donate trips to charities and in most cases, those trips are made up of guys with little to no experience chasing tuna, so I take one or two of my lady crew members along to help. I have to say that this is where things get a little amusing for me at times as the guys don't have a clue about whether the ladies know how to fish or how good they are until we get to the tuna grounds. We have certain things we do to produce fish and the ladies are used to the routine and waste no time in giving instructions to the guys. On one of those charity trips we arrived at the tuna grounds and the sonar was showing the fish were down too deep to troll leaving us with the only option of bringing them up to us. Before I could say anything, my wife grabbed a jig rod and went to working the iron hooking fish, and with a little help, proceeded to get the bite wide open. She continued working the iron putting on a clinic for the guys. Her ability to work the iron and bring fish up was instrumental in putting over 50 fish on the deck on that stop in just three hours, and garnered a lot of kudos by the novice crew acknowledging her efforts so they could enjoy a great day of fishing.

As a guy, I believe you haven't arrived yet as a fisherman until you are willing to acknowledge that women can be good anglers and more importantly, understand why. The reason is simple—in most cases, guys have too much pride to admit they don't know how to do something. The ladies will ask questions, absorbing information like a sponge, and in most cases don't have any bad fishing habits they have to overcome. The drive and determination by women to learn is fueled by their desire to show that they can hold their own while fishing, and that extra effort typically helps them learn the techniques and skills to make them exceptional anglers and worthy crew members on anyone's boat. In most cases, ladies aren't trying to show up us guys, but just want to be treated as equals when onboard and will go the extra mile to learn what they need to do.

LUST is the self-destructive drive for pleasure out of proportion to its worth. When reports of tuna are biting good, I've seen guys strap five-gallon metal jerry cans to the front of open bow river sleds just so they had enough fuel to run 50 miles out to the tuna grounds. They would stop periodically to re-attach a bungee cord to their self-made bomb that would only need one good swell to terminate their adventure and their lives.

When you don't have enough fuel capacity you might also want to reconsider if your boat is seaworthy for that far offshore. If you're having to strap gas cans on the front, chances are you also don't have room for a life raft which then begs the question—what else are you cutting corners on? Do you have any of the right safety equipment for running that far offshore? Weather is one of the biggest issues here, and small boats should not head out in rough seas hoping they will become calmer. Nor should small boats attempt to squeeze a trip in before a forecasted front or predicted storm arrives. Anyone who would put the safety of their crew and themselves at risk to satisfy their lust for chasing tuna is a complete idiot, period.

Instead, pay attention to a variety of weather instruments and forecasts and if it's a go, hitch a ride with a friend on a more capable boat or just charter one. I know it's exciting and exhilarating and holds some level of personal accomplishment to guide your own boat far offshore and out-fish the fleet, but is your lust for this accomplishment really worth your life?

ENVY means resenting the good others receive or even might receive. It is a natural desire to what others possess. Through envying others, we both fail to be happy for them and fail to make the effort to improve ourselves. It's human nature to want what others have, especially when we consider ourselves better qualified and more deserving. Does this scenario sound familiar?

In a fishing situation, you devote a fair amount of time making what you consider to be a good plan, then you run offshore to the tuna grounds and right out of the gate, you start catching fish. One here and one there; you're not lighting it up but you're catching a few, hoping and trying to get the bite wide open. Then the radio crackles with a report of a boat on a wide-open bite and they're hammering them. What happens next? If you're like most folks, you spend the next few minutes beating yourself up for not being in on that bite. You debate trying to figure out where they are and running to that location and you discount what you've been doing. You've been chumming and working your location but have now decided to run to their spot. Typically, you show up just as the bite has died, leaving you frustrated that you wasted the time to pick up and leave what was producing fish, just not at the blistering pace you wanted. Leaving fish to go find more fish is generally counter-productive in the end.

Be honest—how many times has this happened to you? And why? It's tough sticking to your game plan when others are complaining they have no more room for fish.

Envying the catch and accomplishments of others will do nothing to improve your lot in life. Sure, if you are not catching, marking, or seeing any good signs, by all means make a move.

One of the best phrases I've ever heard came when I was a kid working on a neighbor's grass seed farm one summer. I was plowing wheat stubble under and was having a problem with clumps of wheat grass plugging up the plow. The neighbor remarked, "You can't get the field plowed if you don't keep the wheels rolling."

I have found the same thing to be true with tuna—if you chase radio fish all day instead of working a location with good sign you'll be sadly disappointed when you arrive back at the dock. If your lines are not in the water, you're not fishing. A titan of tuna, Tred Barta says, "Be smart and do the work the right way."

GREED. According to Mr. Gecko, "Greed, for lack of a better word, is good!" And it is good when it motivates us to improve ourselves and to improve our lot in life. But when greed turns into the desire for material or monetary gain above all else, it becomes destructive rather than motivational. Very similar to "chasing radio fish," another big sin by anglers is leaving fish they are already catching to go find a greater amount or greater quality to put in the boat. One of the exceptions to this would be during a tournament when you're trying to catch the five heaviest fish for the tournament. Greed and its close cousin Gluttony, go hand in hand.

GLUTTONY includes trying to consume more of anything than you actually need. This not only includes food, but also the finer things in life. You can probably guess where I'm going from here. There's no need to kill every tuna you can get up to the boat and it baffles me why anglers do this just to put up big numbers.

Catching fish to sell commercially so you can pay for your addiction—no problem. But there are those who don't have a clue what they're going to do with all those fish, yet don't want to stop because the bite is so good. It happens quite often with tuna newbies who are still learning. When the adrenaline is pumping because the bite is red hot, stopping is the furthest thing from their minds.

Take the time to have a discussion prior to departure about how many fish everyone wants and if you get into a wide-open bite, keep track of how many you've boated and try to stop when you've landed that last fish. We've had them chomping hot and heavy only to promptly stop when we had what we wanted, leaving them still boiling around the boat. If you still have chum left, dump that overboard and watch the feeding frenzy that ensues—it's quite a sight.

People who have never fished tuna in the Northwest or been involved in a wide-open bite are probably wondering what the heck I'm talking about. Picture 20–30 fish per hour coming over the rail in just two to three hours by four to six anglers. If you're not paying attention you can easily boat more fish than you have fish storage or worse, not enough ice. Tuna not properly bled or iced isn't worth bringing home.

WRATH involves rejecting the love and patience we are supposed to feel for others, opting instead for more violent or hateful interactions. There are no bigger mistakes in life than those caused by anger. The biggest mistake a crew can make is not this sin but it usually leads to this sin.

That mistake is fishing in a crowd.

With thousands of dollars spent on fuel, bait, and motels, and previously invested in boats and tackle, as well as devoting endless hours in pursuit of these great game fish in one of the toughest venues on earth to fish, tensions can run high at times.

When crews are struggling to put fish in the boat, that tension mounts exponentially the tighter and tighter the fleet gets. Whether it begins with boats trolling over the top of each other, or trolling too close to a boat with a bite going, when the bite is slow it doesn't take too long until the explicatives start flying on the radio. But if you really don't mind elevated blood pressure and poor catch rates, go ahead and fight it out in the crowd. The biggest reason that fishing in a crowd is such a sin is that very few boats actually catch very many fish when in a big crowd. Generally, you have a handful of people who do okay, while the others troll endlessly in vain. I'm not sure why fishing in a crowd reduces the catch rate, nor do I care. Maybe all the prop noise going through the water pushes the fish down, or there are simply too many boats fighting over the same fish.

Weekends offer more people the opportunity to get out there and at times I've seen well over 100 boats working a small area with few results. Yet later in the day, when the fleet thins out and most of the frustrated anglers head for home leaving only a few boats, I've seen the fish come up and the bite kick in and go wide open and the remaining boats come home plugged.

You want to talk about anger? Imagine being one of the anglers trolling around and finally going home frustrated, only to log onto a local chat forum Monday afternoon to read about the ones who plugged their boats fishing in the very same spot you trolled all day!

I HOPE NOW THAT YOU'VE SEEN HOW THESE SINS CAN EASILY DERAIL a good day of fishing tuna, you'll be more aware when they start to happen and you can try to avoid them. Otherwise, you might find yourself on the wrong side of the "Dark Side".

Bluefin Mania

WHEN YOU LIVE IN PLACES LIKE THE PACIFIC NORTHWEST, THE winters can be wet and cold leaving us offshore guys wondering what to do or maybe where to go for some sun or a little fishing. How about a tuna fix of another species and one you'll not soon forget? A few years back, I was fortunate enough to get an introduction into a fishery that I bet will get your juices flowing good.

When you think of places like the Outer Banks, names like Oregon Inlet, Nags Head, and Hatteras come to mind. But from Portland, Oregon, there is no short way to get there. The closest airport is Norfolk, Virgina, and then it's a three-hour drive down the coastline and onto the island traveling south through the little coastal communities that dot the Outer Banks.

I had been researching a few charters as I had wanted to go after giant bluefin tuna. Then out of the blue, I received an email that was forwarded to me from a charter skipper who had fished one of my friends on a previous trip. The skipper had sent him a note to say "the bluefin tuna were in."

The first morning I arrived at the Hatteras Village Marina at 6:15 a.m., still road weary and with bloodshot eyes from dealing with the time change, since it was only 3:15 a.m. Oregon time. A brief introduction to Captain Dan Rooks and his first mate Mike Edwards, and we cast the lines and eased out of the slip in the morning darkness. We slowly sneaked our way out of the small harbor moving past magnificent 50 to 60-foot custom-built sport fishing boats. The Carolinas are known for their rich history of boat building with huge flared bows and many are built in a small shed out behind the house. This was one of those boats and the crew had a reputation of knowing the tricks of their trade.

It wasn't long before we dropped lines in the water and started trolling. We put a few skirted ballyhoo lures on the long riggers and added a couple of lines down the middle to fill the spread. It was a nice day on the ocean and we could hear the radio chatter of other charters working the area, all in search of big fish. But after an hour of trolling with no luck, we picked up the lines and ran 10 miles to where half a dozen charters were into the action with multiple hookups reported. We dropped our lines back in and within a few minutes I had my first bluefin tuna on the hook and was doing battle. I quickly realized that I had way too many clothes on and was overheating badly. I was plenty warm for a boat ride, but way overdressed for this workout.

The first day produced constant action once we got into it at around 10 a.m., and by 2 p.m. I was ready to call it a day. I yelled up to the bridge and told Captain Dan I could handle one more and then I'd be done for the day. A few minutes later he obliged, and we had number eight on the hook. The tally now was eight of these big fish landed, with seven of them tagged and then released, with a nice 125-pounder in the box to take home. What a first day—landing fish ranging from 125–250 pounds and doing it in 10–20 minutes each time! If you would have told me before I started that I'd land these brutes in only 10–20 minutes, I would've thought you were crazy. The main key to our quick landings—reels with drags set at 25 pounds at strike, and able to go to 30 pounds maximum drag to finish them off, getting them to the boat. The fish generally made a couple of good runs and then it was gain a little/lose a little, back and forth, before we finally wore them down and got the upper hand on them, depending on the size of the fish.

On the ride back in, I collapsed in a heap on the bench in the salon. I was really in need of a little sleep, but all the action of the first day was replaying over and over in my mind, leaving me too excited. Sleep would just have to wait.

All my muscles were tired and my whole body was exhausted and felt like a noodle. Welcome to Bluefin boot camp. I had a total of three days of fishing with these guys and if this first day was any indication of how things were going to be, I was in for the time of my life.

I was still a little groggy but chipper as I bid good morning to the guys and climbed aboard for another day. We went back to where we left off the day before and after an hour with no action, I was nodding off, sitting on the ice box against the bulkhead. The seas were forecast to be rough in the afternoon but we already had a three-foot wind chop. I was desperately lacking sleep, still tired from the day before, and nothing will put you to sleep quicker than a bobbing boat with no action. At 10:30 a.m. I moved into the salon to have a snack and my thoughts wandered back to the day before. Another hour slowly went by, no bluefin tuna yet, and now it was time for a sandwich. I had just taken my first bite when the sound of singing reels told me we had found the fish. The sandwich got tossed and things were about to get exciting again…

I made a dash for the fighting chair for the first hookup of the day—a triple—and my thoughts were now focused on the task at hand. What a way to start the day! The first fish was barely 100 pounds, but the skipper asked if I would keep it and donate it to the community food bank, so it went in the box. Now it was on to number two and either the activities of the day before were taking their toll or this was a much larger fish. The second fish was kicking my tail, my muscles were screaming and my whole body ached as this battle was an endurance test of strength and will. This fight took longer and after what seemed like an eternity, we were finally able to tag and then release a tuna pushing 300 pounds. It was now onto number three and by now I was hot and overheating again. Mike took my hat off, threw it into the salon, and after a short battle, we were both surprised when the fish came to the boat in just a few minutes. It was a nice fish in the mid-200s but considerably smaller than number two. Mike tagged and released the third fish as I stood up and got out of the fighting chair on wobbly legs.

A few high fives and I turned around making my way to the salon to shed some clothes and cool off. I downed a whole bottle of water while sitting on the bench in the salon with my arms and legs just hanging limp, trying to let them recuperate. I was in a daze trying to fathom what just happened.

My reprieve lasted barely five minutes before the sound of singing clickers brought me out of my stupor and back into the fighting chair. This time, a double, and I set out cranking them in slow and steady…pump, lift and reel…pump, lift and reel. By now my muscles were loosening up and the fish were coming in easier. I was starting to focus more on technique and because my muscles were warmed up, it didn't seem so awkward. Getting into a rhythm and using the fighting harness is a must or you'll be at it all day landing one of these beasts.

The first of a double came in, was tagged, then released, then Mike handed me the second rod. I caught a glimpse of other fish darting back and forth behind the back of the boat. It was incredible—they were swarming all around us and it reminded me of a wide-open bite with albacore. I was working the fish, slow and steady, when out of the corner of my eye I saw a ballyhoo lure sailing past me out over the back of the boat. Suddenly six feet of fish came clear out of the water just 10 feet behind the boat and inhaled the bait. What a sight—another 180-pounder on the hook—and now fish number three was waiting for me. I was now in a groove and focusing on my technique and was bringing these brutes to the boat in less than 15 minutes. Another fish tagged, released, and on to number three then, a moment later, another ballyhoo went sailing past me out over the back of the boat. This bait landed and was in the water less than two seconds when a huge behemoth boiled on it, crashing the bait, and now number four was on the hook and waiting for me. What started out as a double had turned into a four fish hookup.

DEL STEPHENS

Finally, number seven had been tagged and released and I stood up out of the fighting chair and told Captain Dan we needed to break yesterday's eight fish total. He said no problem and I headed to the salon for more water and a break. We didn't even have all the gear out again and we were hooked up again. I took the rod and after a short fight, number eight was now tagged and released. We had established a routine now and things were getting easier. The fish were coming in within a few minutes, were getting tagged, and were being released. I had just enough time to have a snack, a sip of water, and soon the sound of the singing clicker indicated number nine was on the hook. I dashed out of the salon and took up the position in the chair to do battle with our last fish, but the skipper couldn't resist seeing all the fish swarming behind the boat and pitched yet another ballyhoo out the back hooking up one more— meaning it would be a ten-fish day.

In no time I had them up to the boat, one at a time, for Mike to tag and release. It was only 1:30 p.m. and I couldn't believe we had landed 10 fish in just two hours. There was no way we would've achieved this if it had not been for Mike's coaching while I focused on my technique battling these magnificent fish. If you'd told me I could land 10 fish between 150 and 250 pounds all in a matter of two hours, I'd have said, "No way!" but that's just what happened. I felt a sense of satisfaction and a definite feeling of accomplishment and couldn't wait to tell my buddies back home. The skipper and his mate had really put on a show and with some coaching, this angler had experienced way more than I had ever dreamed possible.

The wind had been forecast to build in the afternoon so it was a good time to be headed in for the day. I finished the rest of my sandwich and lay down on the bench as we started the long run back in. We were 55 miles out, 15 miles farther up the coastline than the day before, and now had a sporty sea. But fortunately it was a following sea so we had a relatively smooth ride home.

The next morning, I was at the boat with a smile and Captain Dan took me up to the little café at the marina store for a cup of coffee. He mentioned we were not in a big hurry since we were only going to be running a short distance to where we'd be fishing today. We pulled out of the slip as the sun was breaking over the horizon. It was a beautiful sight shining against the low cloud cover.

We rigged a diver rod for wahoo, a few close lines for yellowfin, and had a couple lines out for bluefin tuna. The morning eeked by slowly with no action, but around noon we picked up a couple of small yellowfin tuna and a black fin tuna that all went in the box. We were trolling over sunken wrecks and underwater structures and after a few passes over the same wreck, the skipper noticed fish about 120 feet below. Captain Dan ask if I knew how to use a butterfly jig and after a nod of acknowledgement said he'd stop the boat over the wreck and I could try my luck. He questioned if I was any good at it and I grinned and chose one of the jig rods in the salon. They had been left by another angler and Dan and his crew didn't really know much about them or how to use them, so hopefully I could contribute a little and maybe they could learn something.

The boat came to a stop. I counted to 120 as the jig was dropping and when I thought I had it about where it should be, I flipped the bail and started the erratic jig retrieve pump and reel action used for bringing up the jig. It only took about three pumps of the rod and I was hooked up and the skipper laughed and commented that he figured I knew what I was doing. Mike put a fighting belt on me and after a brief battle, I landed a nice 20-pound amberjack that went in the box. I showed them the technique again and explained the action used with the jig.

By 3:00 p.m. we had a nice box full of yellowfin tuna to go with the amberjack. We pulled the gear and headed for the harbor. No bluefin tuna today but still a great day on the water. Once back in the slip, I stayed and visited with Captain Dan and Mike covering more details of the techniques and gear used over the last couple of days.

It was a fabulous trip and turned out to be way more than I had expected. We had hit the bluefin tuna at an opportune time the first couple of days and my hosts really put on a show. I came out to learn more about this fishery and they were very willing to share some of their successful techniques. Now I had many pages of notes and couldn't wait to get back to Oregon to give them a try once the summer water temps warmed and the tuna were within reach.

I told them I'd be back and have since made it out to Hatteras a handful of times over the last few years and this past spring made another venture out there to get my offseason tuna fix.

I normally try to make it out there in late March or early April but March was out of the question this time due to scheduling issues. Most years these fish migrate up the Outer Banks of the North Carolina coastline and many years they're gone by the first of April, so I gave my buddy Adam LaRosa a call to see if he still had any of his boats fishing out of Oregon Inlet, in North Carolina. Adam owns Canyon Runner Sport Fishing out of New Jersey and sometimes has a boat down in the Outer Banks during bluefin tuna season. Oregon Inlet is about 50 miles north of Hatteras, where I have been running out of on previous trips, but the bluefin tuna sometimes hang around Oregon Inlet a little longer before jetting on up the coastline. Adam didn't have any of his boats down there this year but recommended Captain Dennis Endee on the A-Salt

Weapon Charters out of Pirates Cove near Manteo, North Carolina. After a few phone calls and emails we had four days of fishing set up for the second week of April. I was stoked! Now, where to stay?

In previous years we've rented large vacation homes at huge offseason discounts but those were farther down in the Outer Banks. So this year we decided to stay at the Oasis Suites, a nice, small boutique hotel, booking a two-bedroom suite with a kitchen just off the living room. It was ideal for this trip since Megan Waltosz wanted to test her wits and grit with these big tuna. She was the only "Team Bad to the Bone" tournament team member who had not been properly introduced to these behemoths and my wife, Weddy, and I owed her a trip. Accommodations were set, so now, how to get there? From our home in Portland, Oregon, the easiest way was to fly to Atlanta, Georgia, then on to Norfolk, Virginia, where we rented an SUV and drove two hours down to Nags Head, North Carolina.

It had been a week since the charter fleet had been out of the tuna grounds due to nasty weather, so the first day of fishing we moved around a lot trying to locate the tuna. Hunting for these fish by yourself would be like looking for a needle in a haystack, but out in the Outer Banks, the charter fleet all hunt together and when one boat gets into them, they all benefit.

Day One - While on the hunt for big fish, we practiced on the little guys catching four yellowfin tuna, one black fin tuna, and a false albacore. Catching football size fish on 80 wides is way more work

than using light tackle.

Day Two - The next day the fleet had moved farther north and after catching a few more yellow footballs, we hooked up on a big boy. Megan was new to the bluefin experience so we gave her the first opportunity in the fighting chair and after a little coaching to get the technique dialed in, it only took 20 minutes before she had the 200-pound fish up to the boat. This one fit the slot length allowing us to keep it so it came onboard. Exhausted with aching arms, she succumbed to the mezzanine bench to get a drink and admire her trophy. Scratch that one off the bucket list!

We were fishing the choppy water where the northerly Gulf Stream met the southerly Labrador Current. This area is rich with sea life and sometimes you never know what might take your bait. On numerous occasions we reeled in a small yellowfin tuna with a small 3 to 4-foot mako shark chomping on the back half of it. It would sometimes take a little persuasion for the shark to leave us with our tuna.

The mezzanine bench seat was a great place to wait watching the rods but any time there were more than 20–30 minutes between fish, the gentle rocking of the boat would put one of us to sleep. But it wasn't long before a singing reel with line peeling off at a blistering pace would bring us instantly to attention, jumping up to go into our routine. The next person up in the rotation would hop in the fighting chair while the others would help to entice another strike, and then clear the lines.

Between the time change and the rocking of the boat, I got in a couple of pretty good naps the first two days.

Day Three - Capt. Dennis went back to where we had caught the bluefin the day before and lines hadn't been in the water more than 20 minutes before we heard that sweet singing sound of line leaving the reel at Mach speed. Weddy was first up in the rotation and found herself battling a 300-pound

class bluefin tuna. Megan kept the chair pointed at the fish and Capt. Dennis maneuvered the boat to try to keep the fish behind the boat. After 40 minutes, Weddy had prevailed and the big fish came alongside the boat. All those four-days-per-week workouts in the gym along with some nice rod handling technique made it a much shorter battle than it could've been. I've seen guys with no technique take an hour to land a much smaller fish. Charter boats in North Carolina are allowed to keep one trophy fish per year exceeding 73 inches and our crew hadn't taken theirs yet so it was decided to keep Weddy's fish.

Barely 20 minutes had elapsed before things heated up again and this time it was a double. My turn in the chair and Capt. Dennis said it acted like a big fish. It dumped line off the 80 wide reel at an incredible speed and finally came to a stop leaving me with less than a ¼ spool of line. The power of these big fish is amazing to watch.

The drags were set at 25 pounds at strike and eventually we'd have the levers pushed to 45 pounds to land them. In some instances we'd move the lever drags up to try to slow them down before being spooled. Most of the time they ran out instead of down even though we were in deep water. After my turn at a 40-minute workout, we released a fish in the 350 pound class. It was warm out on the water that morning and I chose to start out with just a tee shirt, which turned out to be a smart move. I was still sweating when the battle came to an end but nothing like my very first adventure with one of these monsters when I was way overdressed and not in as good of physical shape as today.

Megan had been sitting on the gunwale of the boat keeping the line tight on her fish while I played mine and once it was released, she then moved to the fighting chair and readjusted the bucket harness to fit her. By now she had the technique down and soon we were releasing a 200-pounder.

The day was a blur of constant action. If it wasn't your turn in the chair, you were clearing lines, moving the fighting chair to keep the angler pointed towards the fish, taking photos, and in some cases, giving a warmed up angler a drink of water. Doing battle with a big fish is not just a one-person job. Without the help of a whole team, you'll find yourself on the short end of the deal making it tough to successfully land one of these big fish.

Most of the action happened by 1 p.m. making for a quiet afternoon and allowing for a few more naps. By the end of the day, we had each landed two fish for a total of six bluefin tuna. We had three fish over 300 pounds, keeping one of them, and another three fish in the 170 to 250-pound range. What a day—I couldn't believe the size class of fish we were catching! In previous trips out to Hatteras, I had caught fish in the 100 to 300-pound class but it was rare to have one over 250 pounds. We had just caught three over 300 pounds and our smallest fish was close to 170 pounds.

Once back at the dock we took a few more pictures before heading back to the Oasis Suites where we cleaned up before venturing over to Ortega'z Southwestern Grill & Wine Bar in nearby Manteo. Later that evening I savored the end of a great day with a nice bourbon and good cigar out on the deck while reminiscing about the events of a fantastic day. Tired but happy sleep came easy.

Day Four - The next morning Capt. Dennis eased the big boat out of the slip from Pirates Cove as we made our way down the causeway to start the last day of our fishing. We passed Oregon Inlet and headed east to the Gulf Stream. Rain was threatening but we didn't care. We were prepared to give it our all on the final day of what would become one of the most memorable days I've ever had on the water. We ran 90 minutes to the Gulf Stream and Guy, our deck hand, wasted no time deploying the lines. I was still putting on my raingear bibs when the reel started singing. Hopping on one leg and fighting a bobbing boat, I made my way to the fighting chair and buckled in for the fight. I was first up in the fighting chair but right away I could tell it was a much smaller fish than I'd been tangling with the previous days and within 20 minutes it was alongside the boat. The smallest bluefin tuna of the trip and it was still 165 pounds. After fighting 300-pounders the day before, this was a walk in the park.

Lines went back out and we were back on the hunt. I had just enough time to get a snack before the reels were singing again. This time another double.

Megan was first up in the chair so Weddy camped out on the gunwale and kept the line tight on her fish while Megan worked hers to submission before releasing another nice fish in the 250 pound class. Weddy moved to the fighting chair and we handed her the rod, locking in the harness for what turned out to be the longest battle of the trip. The fish had almost spooled her and didn't seem to be showing any signs of letting up. Capt. Dennis backed up on the fish to reclaim half a mile of line that looked like it was running off over the horizon. Slowly the line winched back onto the reel and after a long 40 minutes, we saw the monofilament top shot, now another 250 yards to go. Weddy worked to gain more ground. The fish would move to one side, then the other, and Capt. Dennis would maneuver the boat to keep the fish behind the boat. Back and forth, side to side, we'd go. Guy was constantly watching to make sure the line never touched the boat. Early in the fight, Weddy had pushed the drag to 45 pounds and this fish wasn't showing much sign of giving in. She'd gain a little then lose a little. This give and take went on for another 15 minutes before we saw the 130 pound Seaguar fluorocarbon leader.

Once Guy was able to leader the fish, he was able to put a little more pressure on the fish, finally working it to the side of the boat where we were able to get a few pictures before releasing a fish well over 500 pounds.

By noon we had landed a small 165 pound fish which would eventually be donated to the Nags Head food bank and we had released four others including the big bruiser Weddy had battled. The ocean was turning ugly on us and the seas were building so we decided to call it a day and run for home.

Four days of fishing just off the outer banks of North Carolina had produced some incredible action landing 15 yellowfin tuna and 12 big bluefin tuna. We also made some new friends along with some fantastic memories.

If you're thinking of giving it a go, the bluefin tuna can show up any time from November through April but the last couple of seasons, the best times have been late February through March. The weather is generally a little better in late March, but you need to be prepared for wintertime conditions should a cold front move in. Just layer up because one of these big fish will heat you up in no time.

Getting into a wide-open albacore bite will get your blood pumping but when winter comes and the albacore have left, chasing big bluefin tuna is a great way to get a fix until the warm summer waters fill in and the albacore returns.

Tight lines!

ABOUT THE AUTHOR

MANY BELIEVE THAT CAPTAIN DEL STEPHENS, AKA "TUNA DOG," was born with fins, not hands. He's been an avid angler since he was old enough to handle a fishing rod. His love for fishing and boating continues to grow deeper with every day he spends on the water.

Del's angling obsession began on the high lakes of Oregon's Cascade Mountains stalking monster lake trout and kokanee. It was here the brilliant colors of the early morning sunrise enlightened his uncompromising love of the outdoors and the challenge of outsmarting the elusive fish below.

From his home in Portland, Oregon, his journeys have expanded to fisheries throughout the west and around the world. He's caught marlin, dorado, and roosterfish in Mexico, chased sailfish and tarpon in Costa Rica, landed giant sea run brown trout in Tierra Del Fuego, boated big wahoo in the Bahamas, and makes an annual trek to pursue monster bluefin tuna out of Hatteras, North Carolina. While the local waters of the Willamette and Columbia River lure him frequently, it's the offshore waters of the deep blue that have emerged as his greatest passion. Only the weather will stop him from running offshore during the spring, summer, and fall in search of tuna, salmon, and halibut.

Del captains BAD TO THE BONE, a 33-foot Hydra Sports center console powered by triple 300 horsepower Mercury Verados equipped with the latest state-of-the-art Garmin electronics, including radar, for chart mapping and fish finding. He holds a Coast Guard 100 Ton Masters license and was a charter captain for many years but now primarily focuses on fishing offshore tournaments, pleasure fishing, and giving seminars. Del's easygoing attitude, natural fishing abilities, and love for the sport create an environment for him to share his knowledge with others. He's used to being on the podium in front of a microphone and is a regular speaker at sport shows and gives 20 to 30 seminars every year at retailers, sport shows, boat shows, and special events. He's a regular speaker during the Saltwater Sportsmen's Show in Salem, Oregon, and was the marquee speaker and master of ceremonies during the 2013 Saltwater Sportsmen's Show. He's one of the featured seminar speakers at the Washington Sportsmen's Show in Puyallup, Washington, as well as the Pacific Northwest Sportsmen's Show in Portland, Oregon. In 2014 his tuna seminars were called the "Dark Side Tour" and were a huge hit on the West Coast.

In the last nine years he has worked at helping to build the Oregon Tuna Classic Tournament Series into one of the largest charity fishing tournaments on the West Coast, serving as the chairman for eight years. The tournament series draws over 1,200 participants from five western states with all the proceeds going to help the hungry and those less fortunate in Oregon and Washington coastal communities.

Honored by the Governor in 2010, Del received the Outstanding Oregon Tourism Volunteer Award for the impact the tournaments made on the local coastal communities. Those efforts were also acknowledged in 2010 by the Bohemian Foundation when he received the e-Chievement Award "celebrating those who are making a positive difference in their communities and beyond." In 2012 he received the Hall of Fame Award from the Oregon Coalition for Educating Anglers for all the years of service and support he has given them.

Del is the captain of Team Bad To The Bone, a Portland, Oregon, based offshore tournament team comprised of five members, who are a perennial contenders any time they are on the water in pursuit of big game. A mixture of intellectual young energy and mature years of experience has enabled his team to grace the podium a record 13 times in the last seven years during the Oregon Tuna Classic Tournament Series. They won the series in 2012 and received an official invitation to compete in the Offshore World Championships held in Costa Rica in April 2013. Del is well known and highly regarded as a leader in the offshore fishing circles on the West Coast.

For more than 25 years, Del has using and endorsing products for DAIWA, Garmin, Mercury, Fish Trap Lures, Lamiglas, Eat Me Lures, Rapala, Williamson, Ballyhood, Seaguar, TUF-Line, Terrafin, and Gamakatsu. He maintains affiliations with Berkley, Mustang Survival, Hot Fish, and Yakima Bait and Lamiglas markets a "Tuna Dog Series" of offshore rods with his logo and endorsement.

Del has graced the covers and been featured in numerous magazines including *Sport Fishing Magazine*, *Saltwater Sportsman Magazine*, *Western Outdoors Magazine*, *Outdoor Life Magazine*, *Northwest Sportman Magazine*, CCA's *Tide Magazine* and he's been on nationally broadcast television and radio programs including *America's Outdoor Journal*, *Outdoor GPS*, *ESPN Outdoors TV* and *The Joy of Fishing*. He's an occasional guest host on *Northwest Wild Country TV* and sports radio show, and anchors the 13-week *Tuna Nation* segment during the summer and fall months. He writes articles for numerous magazines and some of those articles are featured on his personal website www.tunadogoffshore.com. His new book *The Dark Side: One Man's Journey to the 125 Line and Back* will be in bookstores and on Amazon in winter, 2016.

Google Del Stephens for more information on him and his tournament team, and contact him at:

Phone: 503-539-0006

Email: pointman40@hotmail.com

Facebook: https://www.facebook.com/del.stephens.3

Twitter: @tunadog33

CPSIA information can be obtained at www.ICGtesting.com
Printed in the USA
BVIW12n0243250118
505534BV00012B/65